THE PLACE OF SUFFERING

The Place of Suffering

by

JOHN FERGUSON

*Dean and Director of Studies
in Arts, The Open University*

JAMES CLARKE & CO. LTD.
CAMBRIDGE & LONDON

First Published 1972
© John Ferguson

Published by James Clarke & Co. Ltd.,
7 All Saints Passage, Cambridge, U.K.,
and distributed by Trade Counter Ltd.,
11-14 Stanhope Mews West,
London, S.W.7

Printed in Great Britain by
The Camelot Press Ltd., London and Southampton

FOR
MY MOTHER

Contents

Contents

1

The Witness of the Pre-classical World

The great feature of life in the temperate zones is its seasonal variations. As the Roman poet Horace put it, discerning a parable of man's destiny,

> Thaw follows frost: hard on the heel of spring
>   Treads summer sure to die, for hard on hers
> Comes autumn, with his apples scattering;
>   Then back to wintertide, when nothing stirs.
>
> (O 4, 7, 9–12: tr. A. E. HOUSMAN)

Wintertide when nothing stirs. There is a cycle of action and passion, growth and decay, life and death, and it was natural for man to make a myth of this. All the world over we have seasonal myths of the death of the god or goddess of the year; sometimes it blurs and blends with the burial of the corn-ear in the ground before it can fructify: "Verily, verily, I say unto you, Except a corn of wheat fall into the ground and die, it abideth alone: but if it die it bringeth forth much fruit" (*John* 12.12). It is here that we first encounter any serious treatment of the fact of suffering.

The oldest story of this kind comes from Sumer. There the great fertility goddess was known as Inanna, the queen of heaven. Her husband and love was the shepherd-god Dumuzi. Not content with ruling heaven the goddess yearned for power over the lower world.

> From the "great above" she set her mind toward the "great below",

> The goddess, from the "great above" she set her mind toward
>   the "great below",
> Inanna, from the "great above" she set her mind toward the
>   "great below".
>
> My lady abandoned heaven, abandoned earth,
>   To the nether world she descended,
> Inanna abandoned heaven, abandoned earth,
>   To the nether world she descended,
> Abandoned lordship, abandoned ladyship,
>   To the nether world she descended.

The queen of the "great below" was Inanna's bitterly hostile sister Ereshkigal, the sovereign of death. Inanna, fearing her fate, told her vizier Ninshubur, her "knight of true words", if she should fail to return, to start mourning her, and to go and plead with the gods and goddesses, "Let not the maid Inanna be put to death in the nether world." Then Inanna left the vizier and walked boldly up to the gate of the palace below, the "lapis lazuli mountain", and called for the gate to be opened. She made no attempt to conceal her identity, but tried to conceal her mission. The gatekeeper reported to Ereshkigal.

> Then Ereshkigal bit her thigh, was filled with wrath,
> Says to Neti, her chief gatekeeper:
> "Come, Neti, chief gatekeeper of the nether world,
> The word which I command you, neglect not,
> Of the seven gates of the nether world, lift their bolts,
> Of its one palace Gangir, the 'face' of the nether world,
>   press open its doors,
> Upon her entering,
> Bowed low, let her be brought naked before me."

So, as Inanna passed through each of the seven gates she was stripped of some of her finery, and brought naked to her sister's presence, where sentence of death was pronounced on her.

> The pure Ereshkigal seated herself upon her throne,
> The Anunnaki, the seven judges, pronounced judgment before
>   her,
> She fastened her eye upon her, the eye of death,

Spoke the word against her, the word of wrath,
Uttered the cry against her, the cry of guilt,
The sick woman was turned into a corpse,
The corpse was hung from a rail.

Meanwhile her vizier carried out his instructions, and after three days started mourning. Some of the gods refused to help, but Enki was sympathetic:

"What now has happened to my daughter! I am troubled.
What now has happened to Inanna! I am troubled.
What now has happened to the queen of all lands! I am troubled.
What now has happened to the hierodule of heaven! I am troubled."

Enki formed from his fingernail two curious creatures called *kurgarru* and *kalaturru* and sent them to sprinkle the dead Inanna with the food and water of life. This revived her, but her trials were not yet over.

Inanna is about to ascend from the nether world,
The Anunnaki seized her, saying:
"Who of those who have descended to the nether world
    ever ascends unharmed from the nether world!
If Inanna would ascend from the nether world,
Let her give someone as her substitute."

So Inanna ascended, escorted by ferocious demons, to seek a substitute. She first went to the cities of Umma and Bad-Tibara. Their protecting deities prostrated themselves humbly in sackcloth before her, and she spared them. She then came to Kullab, whose protecting god was her husband Dumuzi. Dumuzi did not prostrate himself humbly.

Dumuzi put on a noble robe, he sat high on his throne. Inanna loosed the demons on him.

She fastened the eye upon him, the eye of death,
Spoke the word against him, the word of wrath,
Uttered the cry against him, the cry of guilt:
"As for him, carry him off."
The pure Inanna gave the shepherd Dumuzi into their hands.

Dumuzi prayed for rescue to the sun-god Utu, but though the story breaks off there, we may assume that the prayer was unavailing.

This is a story of great interest. First, it is plainly a myth symbolizing the seasonal cycle. To put it differently, death is the condition of resurrection, and in this myth we have the first resurrection story. Secondly, it gives a picture of life in which cruelty and mercy are commingled. Some gods help, others do not. Inanna herself shows mercy on the gods who prostrate themselves, but is merciless to Dumuzi. Thirdly, there is the doctrine of substitutionary sacrifice, but in this legend the substitution is not offered freely and voluntarily.

The Babylonian myths followed a closely similar pattern for most of the story. The queen of heaven is called Ishtar, and Dumuzi has become Tammuz. In the earliest Babylonian version Tammuz played no part apart from a mysterious reference at the end. Ishtar descended to the underworld; the conversation with the keeper of the gate remained, but Ishtar's approach was fiercer and less cozening:

> Gatekeeper, open your gate,
> Open your gate that I may enter!
> If you do not open your gate, so that I cannot enter,
> I will smash the door, I will shatter the bolt,
> I will smash the doorpost, I will move the doors,
> I will raise up the dead, eating the living,
> So that the dead will outnumber the living.

The stripping of Ishtar also remained. In her nakedness Ishtar lost control of herself before Ereshkigal and attacked her furiously. Ereshkigal in retaliation unleashed a pack of diseases upon her sister. Meanwhile on earth trees and flowers would not grow, men and flocks remained barren.

> The bull springs not upon the cow;
> The ass impregnates not the jinny;
> In the street the man impregnates not the maiden.

The gods were appalled, and Ea formed a being destined to be

sacrificed, and then on arrival in the underworld to command
Ereshkigal to give him the water of life.

> When the goddess Ereshkigal heard these words,
> She struck her thigh, she gnawed her fingers.

She cursed the gods' envoy, telling him that he would receive
nothing to eat and drink except "the scraps from the gutter and
the water from the town-conduits". But she could not resist his
request, and poured on Ishtar the water of life. Ishtar thus returned
through the seven gates, recovering her accoutrements as she
went, and life was restored to earth. The vegetation-myth is
clearer here than in the Sumerian version, but both stories are
essentially the same, and in fact the Sumerian liturgies show the
desolation.

There is another version of the story, which is more familiar.
In this version, which is fully described only in a later period, but
which seems from the liturgies to reach back into Sumerian times,
and which may be alluded to in the Babylonian myth, it is
Tammuz who dies first, and with his death desolation and barren-
ness fall on the earth. Ishtar's descent to the underworld, which is
so graphically told in the myth that it could not be lost, then
became the goddess's journey to rescue her love, who returns in
triumph. This myth explained the two great festivals—the
mourning for the death of the year, the joy for its rebirth. It was
the former which attracted the attention of foreigners. "Then he
brought me to the door of the gate of the lord's house which was
toward the north; and behold, there sat women weeping for
Tammuz" (*Ezek.* 8.14). The Greek Plutarch tells a curious story
of how a ship, steered by a sailor named Thamous, was passing a
particular point when he heard his name called and the message
"Great Pan is dead". It is almost certain that what he heard was
the liturgy of mourning: "Tammuz the All-Great [in Greek
Pan-megas] is dead." It has been reasonably supposed that the
change in the myth was due to the migration of the Sumerian
from a mountain-region to the Mesopotamian plains, and the
change of their economy from pastoral to agricultural. That
Tammuz and Ishtar belong to the period before the migration is

shown in that they are represented by fir-trees, which are not found in the Mesopotamian delta.

Similar myths are found all over the Middle East. In the Ugaritic myth there is a conflict between Baal, the god of fertility, and Mot, a vegetation-god who becomes god of the underworld. Baal refuses tribute to Mot, and Mot humbles him. Baal is found dead, though we do not know from what cause, and is in the underworld. On earth there is drought and famine. Baal's sister Anath mourns him, and wanders in search of him. She finds Mot, seizes him, "splits him with her sword, winnows him with her fan, burns him with fire, grinds him in her hand-mill, and sows him in the ground"—all appropriate fates for a corn-deity. What follows is obscure, but it is clear that there can be no successor to Baal. It appears that Baal and Mot are both resurrected, and enter on a new struggle which ends in reconciliation.

The Syrian version is the most familiar. The young god is here called Adonis, which means "the lord". He is the direct descendant of Tammuz with some admixture of Baal. In the Greek version which we possess, the fertility-goddess is called Aphrodite; she is of course Inanna-Ishtar. In the simplest version of the story, the child Adonis is so beautiful that Aphrodite puts him in a casket to keep him for herself when he shall grow up; she entrusts the casket to the goddess of the underworld. But the latter opens the casket and falls in love with Adonis herself. There is conflict between the goddesses, as a result of which Adonis spends half of the year on earth and half in the underworld. The commoner story tells how Adonis, of mature age and beloved by the goddess, insists on going hunting, and is killed by a boar. In yet another version (where the god usually appears as Attis) he castrates himself and bleeds to death under a pine tree; here the theme of fertility is strong, as is the theme of suffering. Each year he was mourned. "It seems," writes Saglio, "that nothing was lacking which normally took place at funerals: neither the oiling nor toilet of the dead, nor the exhibition of the body, funeral offerings and communal repasts. Images of Adonis in wax and terracotta were placed before the entrance or on the terraces of houses. Women crowded round them or carried them through the town, wailing and beating their breasts with every sign of the deepest grief. They danced and chanted dirges to the strident sound of short flutes—called *giggros* or *giggras*—which the Phoenicians used for their funeral ceremonies." The river Adonis, today the Nahr Ibrahim, when the waters were high, would run red with particles of haematite. This was believed to be the annual outpouring of Adonis's blood.

2

Seasonal myths apart, there is evidence of some speculation about the problem of suffering in the Mesopotamian texts. It has been persuasively suggested by a distinguished Dutch scholar that this is found back in the Sumerian period in the third millennium B.C. The view is based upon two texts which are full of obscurities, and cannot be said to have been firmly established. In the later Akkadian tablets it is clear.

The most striking example is an anticipation of the *Book of Job*, though without the latter's glorious imagery or theological profundity. It is often called *The Poem of the Righteous Sufferer*, and it probably dates from somewhere around the middle of the second millennium B.C. It consists of a monologue of some five hundred lines put into the mouth of an anonymous Babylonian noble. He begins: "I will praise the lord of wisdom", and goes on to tell how despite a life of upright piety he was abandoned by the gods and fell into disfavour with the king and court. The magicians and medicine-men could do nothing for him. Yet he had tried to live in such a way as to secure the approval of the gods.

> Would that I knew that these things found favour with the god.
> That which is good to oneself is an insult to the god;
> That which is of ill repute in a man's own heart is good to the god.
> Who knows the opinion of the gods in the midst of heaven?

Now, on top of his other disasters, he is struck down by illness. A swarm of devils surround him, and his subsequent symptoms have been diagnosed as malaria, dysentery, tuberculosis and paralysis. In this state he falls into a restless sleep, and in his sleep dreams.

First comes a young man of noble bearing, but our text is faulty, and the purport of his words is lost. He is followed by another young man who performs rites of exorcism over the sufferer. Next comes a woman dressed as a queen or goddess, with a promise of salvation, followed by a priest carrying a tablet with a promise of restored prosperity from the great god Marduk himself. In face of Marduk's favour calamity disappears. The devils are driven back to hell; the disease is cured; the sufferer returns to royal favour and to the approbation of his fellows. He goes for Thanksgiving to Marduk's temple. Unfortunately the last tablet of the series is missing, unless, as some people think, we have fragments of his triumphal entry into the temple in his restored prosperity. We do not know for certain how the poem ended, but it is unlikely that the last tablet contained any startling surprises.

A second work of some importance is known as *The Babylonian Theodicy*. This is a complex literary composition, consisting in full of 27 verses of 11 lines each. In each verse all the lines begin with the same syllable, and the 27 syllables spell out "I am Saggil-kinam-ubbib the incantation priest, worshipper of the god and the king". Saggil-kinam-ubbib was exercised over the problem of suffering, and his composition is a dialogue between a sufferer and his friend.

> My friend, your mind is a spring whose source is unfailing.
> It is the accumulation of the mighty sea, of which there is no diminution.
> I will pose a question to you; heed my saying!
> Pay attention for a moment! Listen to my words!
> My bodily grace is hidden, distress overclouds me;
> My luck has passed me by, my luxury has passed;
> My vigour has turned to weakness; my splendour has come to an end;
> Lamentation and grief have disfigured my face.
> Rations from my farm are far from adequate for me;
> My wine, the life of mankind, is a long way from satisfying my need.
> Is there a time of favour arranged for me? I would like to know the way to get it.

Saggs has summarized the main contents in a way which gives a clear notion of the argument.

Sufferer: I was a posthumous child and my mother died in childbed, leaving me an orphan.

Friend: Death is the lot of all people.

Sufferer: I am in bad health physically, miserable and not well off.

Friend: The gods finally reward the pious.

Sufferer: There are cases of people prospering without piety: I have been pious without prospering.

Friend: We do not understand the ways of the gods. The impious who prosper temporarily will finally get their deserts.

Sufferer: According to my observation this has not been the case.

Friend: It is blasphemy to dispute the decisions of the gods.

At each point the theory of the divine governance of the world is countered by an appeal to the facts of life. The conclusion is that justice is not to be found among men, and this is because the gods have made them unjust.

Another curious work, peripheral but not irrelevant to our purpose, is the satirical *Dialogue of Pessimism.* This is an amusing interchange between a master and an obsequious slave, who agrees with his master however the latter contradicts himself.

"Slave, make yourself agreeable!" "Yes, sir, yes."
"Fetch water for my hands straightaway and give it to me,
so that I may make a sacrifice to my god." "Do so, sir, do so!
That man who makes sacrifices to his god, his heart is content;
He makes investment upon investment."
"No, slave, I will not make a sacrifice to my god at all." "Don't
do so, sir, don't do so!
As to a god, you can train him so that he keeps trotting behind
you like a dog.
Whether it is rites he wants from you . . . or anything else."

After a series of such tos and fros the master asks the direct question, What course of action really is worthwhile?, and the slave gives the direct answer.

"To have my neck and your neck broken
And us thrown into the river—that is good!"

This dialogue is not a serious work, and it is not explicitly concerned with the problem of suffering, but there seems an underlying conviction that life is meaningless, and to be escaped from.

There is nothing profound in this Wisdom literature from Babylon. But we can say that suffering was regarded as a theological and moral problem. The simple answer was that suffering is the god's punishment upon unrighteousness, but this was falsified by the facts. In face of this we have seen three answers given. The first is, "Wait. It will be all right in the end." The second, "Injustice is written so deeply on the heart of life that it must come from the gods themselves." The third is "Life is meaningless." None of these answers could satisfy, but the problem was raised.

3

Babylonian medical practice depended upon a belief that sin and suffering were interconnected. In other words, illness was a visitation by a demon, who had been enabled to enter the patient because of some offence the patient had committed. To lay bare the offence was one method, and ultimately the best, of exorcizing the demon, though the demon could sometimes be forced out by physical means, such as induced vomiting. Symptoms and sins were swiftly correlated, and regular formulae for treatment presented. When the symptoms proved harder to identify, the priest or "medicine-man" would read over to the patient a list of offences which he might have committed, knowingly or unknowingly, in the hope of identifying the demon successfully. If all else failed the priest was reduced to an attempt to bribe the demon to leave the patient.

One interesting element in medical practice was the belief that suffering could be transferred. An animal might be taken, and identified with the patient point by point, in the hope presumably that the demon would be misled into transferring his attentions to the animal. The fact that the animal was often a pig throws some light upon the story of the Gadarene swine. Sometimes an inanimate object, such as a reed, was used.

This doctrine of substitution and of transferred punishment or suffering is of some importance. We have seen it already in Sumerian times in the willingness of the Anunnaki to accept Dumuzi as a substitute for Inanna. This belief in substitutionary suffering was used to protect the king. Just as a reed might act as a substitute for a patient, so the royal robes might act as a substitute for the king. At other times a dummy would be used, dressed in the king's clothes. But when the omens signified that danger was imminent and acute, a human substitute was provided, from among the courtiers or palace officials. The king ruled behind the scenes; the substitute appeared in public. It might be that the omens signified death. In that case the substitute faced the danger publicly. A death in the course of things among the courtiers was regarded as fulfilling the omen. But if no death occurred and the omens continued baleful, then the substitute might be put to death; this was called "going to meet his destiny". We have a full account of an occasion when this actually took place. It was in the reign of Esarhaddon, and the substitute was named Damai. He had a period enjoying the pomp and circumstance of an absolute monarch; but, as the omens grew grimmer, he and his concubine were put to death, and mourned and buried with full ceremony, to complete the expiation.

4

Egypt provides one celebrated seasonal myth of suffering. This is the story of Osiris. The narrative, although with tendentious interpretation, is well told by Plutarch. Osiris was of supernatural origin; at his birth a voice was heard calling, "The Lord of All has come into the world." Osiris married his sister Isis; his brother Set or Typhon married another sister Nephthys. Osiris reigned over the Egyptians and reclaimed them from savagery, gave them laws and taught them religion. They had previously been canni-bals. Now with the help of Isis he introduced wheat and barley, and also the brewing of beer from barley (for which he was loaded with the gratitude of the nations). The evil Set, with seventy-two others, plotted against him. The queen of Ethiopia made a highly ornamented coffin, to be given to the person it would fit; it had been secretly made to Osiris's measurements. When Osiris climbed in, the conspirators shut the lid, nailed it down, soldered it with molten lead and flung it into the Nile. It was washed out to sea and floated ashore at Byblos in Syria, where an erica-tree shot up enclosing it, which the king made a pillar of his palace.

Meanwhile Isis, having given birth to the younger Horus, was wandering disconsolately. She experienced various adventures, including death by scorpions and identification with birds, and eventually reached Byblos, where the queen took pity on her sorrow and employed her as a baby-nurse. So she was able to rescue the body, but while she was visiting Horus, Set stole it again and cut it into fourteen pieces. These she rescued and buried separately, with a view to bringing them together again by magic power, all but the sex-organ, which could not be recovered; so she had a model of that made (an aetiological explanation of the use of a phallic symbol in religious processions). Horus conquered Set in three battles, and Isis gave birth to Harpocrates, who is evidently a doublet of Horus.

To this myth Egyptian sources make some important additions, notably the lament for Osiris by Isis and Nephthys which is closely parallel to the lament for Tammuz or Adonis, and the resurrection of Osiris to reign as king over the dead, standing as a pledge of future resurrection available for all men. There is an interesting fragment of a hymn to Osiris dating from the Middle Kingdom, which shows something of the picture of Isis:

> His sister protected him,
> It is she who expelled his enemies and averted misfortune,
> Who repulsed the adversary by the magic formulas of her mouth,
> Whose tongue is skilful,
> Whose mouth is never lacking in words,
> Who wields authority well,
> It is she, Isis, the just, who protects her brother,
> Who seeks him without wearying,
> Who in mourning traverses the whole land without respite before
>   finding him,

Who gives shade with her feathers
And wind with her wings.
It is she who praises her brother,
Who relieves the weakness of him who is tired,
Who receives his seed and gives birth to his heir,
Who nurtures the child in solitude,
Without anyone's knowing where she is.

Here Isis partakes of the character of the suffering redeemer. More light is shown by some of the rituals. For example the ritual associated with the burial of the human dead was said to be a replica of the actions of the mourners over Osiris. Every mummy was in some sense identified with Osiris, and the dead man was called by the name Osiris; the female mourners became Isis and Nephthys. Isis became a universal goddess, the myriad-named, and all the gods and goddesses of the ancient world were regarded as adumbrations of her power. Thus there came to be a universal hope of future life. That this was associated with the fertility of the earth is also clear. Sirius which appears at the time of the rising waters of the Nile, upon which the fruitfulness of Egypt depends, was called "the star of Isis". Furthermore, it was a custom of the Egyptian corn-reapers to weep over the first sheaf cut and to call upon Isis. The Greek historian Herodotus tells us that at Sais in Lower Egypt once a year the sufferings of Osiris were commemorated as a mystery on the lake by night. His account is frustratingly brief, but we know that they carried out the image of a cow (and that this stood for Isis searching), and that all the houses were lit up, suggesting that this was a festival in which all the dead were commemorated. Plutarch also describes a festival which took place from November 13 to 16 where a gilt cow swathed in black was exhibited. On the third day the people went down to the sea, the priests carrying a shrine with a golden casket. Into this they would pour fresh water, and the people raised the shout "Osiris is found". They then took some vegetable mould, moistened it with water, mixed it with spices and incense, and made a small moon-shaped image, which they robed and decorated. The Christian Lactantius provides another account, telling how the priests used to beat their breasts and lament, imitating the search of Isis for her lost son Osiris, and how their sorrow was turned to joy when the jackal-headed god, Anubis, produced a small boy, the living representative of the lost and found god; there is here some confusion between Osiris and Horus, but the account is basically sound. Another piece of evidence comes from a long epigraphic account of an eighteen-day festival, dating from the Ptolemaic period. The account is probably confused and certainly confusing, and it is likely that there is a conflation of varying versions of the festivals from different districts. What is certain is that the festival represented three different periods: when Osiris is dead, dismembered and reconstituted. There were ceremonies of ploughing and sowing to begin the festival; images of vegetable mould were used; and much was made of the burial ceremonies. To this evidence may be added a remarkable series of bas-reliefs, representing in a sequence of scenes, comic-strip-wise, the dead god lying swathed as a mummy, gradually raising himself until he is free from the bier, and finally appearing between the guardian wings of the faithful Isis, while a male figure holds up a *crux ansata*, the symbol of eternal life. In another representation in the temple of Isis at Philae we see the dead body of Osiris with stalks of corn springing from it. A priest is watering the stalks from a pitcher, and an accompanying inscription reads: "This is the form of him whom one may not name, Osiris of the mysteries, who springs from the returning waters." Lastly, we must note some very remarkable effigies of Osiris, sometimes made of vegetable mould, always stuffed with corn, and buried in Egyptian graves or found between the legs of mummies.

Osiris thus became the god of the dead. He was the judge; in his resurrection lay the promise of life in those blessed fields where, it is significantly asserted, the corn grows to unbelievable heights and the rivers were always filled with water. So to Osiris prayers were spoken and offerings made in the hope of a blessed life beyond the grave. He was lord of eternity. So the dead man was addressed: "O thou who canst not move like Osiris, O thou whose limbs cannot move like those of Osiris, let not thy limbs be without movement; let them not suffer corruption; let them not pass away; let them not decay; let them be fashioned for me as if I myself were Osiris." The priestly comment says: "If the dead man knows this paragraph he shall never suffer corruption in the underworld." For it was believed that in the underworld he would face the judgment of Osiris where he would have to swear his innocence, and where his heart would be weighed in the scales against the symbol of justice.

The end of this is clear. This is a vegetation myth; the corn dies and rises again. Suffering and death are the condition of new life. The believer is identified with Osiris. One of the Coffin Texts (4, 330) expresses this: "I live, I die, I am Osiris. I have come out of you, I have entered into you, I have become fat in you, I have grown in you, I have fallen into you, I have fallen on to my side. The gods live on me. I live, I grow as Nepre [the corn god] who takes out the venerable ones with himself. Geb [the earth god] has hidden me, I live, I die; I am the barley—I shall not perish." Or again: "As truly as Osiris lives, so truly shall his followers live; as truly as Osiris is not dead he shall die no more; as truly as Osiris is not annihilated he shall not be annihilated."

5

In our Egyptian sources we also have from an early period and in fragmentary form some meditations upon misfortune, dating no doubt from periods of disaster, such as the breakdown of the Old Kingdom. The most remarkable of these is the so-called *Dispute with His Soul of One who is Tired of Life*. The man stands apart from his soul, and they discuss together. The beginning of the tract is missing, but it is clear that he has met with calamity upon calamity, and wishes to escape from life. His soul first supported him in this, then threatened to abandon him in death, but in the end stood by him. Some of the dialogue is frankly obscure, and has generated a pile of scholarly literature *pyramidum altius*, but the poems, though peculiar in form, are clear in meaning and eloquent in their expression of the human predicament; the first deals with the man's desolation, the second with corruption in society, the third with the prospect of death as health, beauty and freedom, and the fourth with the life after death as the life of power and knowledge. No explanation is given for suffering in life, but there is remedy beyond the tomb.

A little later, but plainly from the same period, is a fragmentary prophetic pronouncement by a seer named Ipuwer. This depicts a period of chaos and corruption when the doorkeepers say "Let us go and plunder" and the workers refuse to do their jobs, when the heart is violent, plague stalks the land, the river is blood, the buildings are laid waste with fire, the crocodiles are glutted, laughter has perished, and men say, "I wish I were dead." In a new poem the seer describes worse calamities in which the power of the king himself is destroyed and revolution is rampant. In other poems he seems to have turned to advocate constructive policies, active resistance to the enemies of the state and restoration of the worship of the gods, with a vision of the land once more at peace, and prosperous, with the people blissfully drunk! Here the conclusion is that the remedy for suffering lies in our own hands, and self-help and prayer will save the day.

From about 1900 B.C. comes the meditation of Khekheperre-sonbu, a priest of Heliopolis. This is a much more artificial work, written with stylistic deliberation, and as only the Introduction is preserved it is not easy to draw any conclusions. It is a period of public affliction, in which he somewhat self-righteously shares; part of the burden of his complaint is that other people either do not know or do not care what is happening. To that extent it seems that his solution is much that of Ipuwer. Suffering is not irremediable, but can be met with an active care.

The last of these, *The Eloquent Peasant*, is in some ways the most interesting, though less to our immediate point. In fantastic language a peasant complains, in nine denunciations, of the exactions of the Establishment; comparison has been made with Amos or Deutero-Isaiah, justly, in that, like Amos, the peasant came from outside the centre of government. The denunciation is clear, forthright and eloquent. "The magistrates do evil, the well-ordered speech is partial. They that give hearing, steal. . . . He that should give air to breathe, takes away breath . . . the arbitrator is a spoiler . . .; he that should combat wrong, himself does evil. . . . He that measures the corn-heaps, converts to his own use; he that fills up for another, apportions too little to his intimates; he that should lead according to law, gives orders to rob. Who then shall redress evil, when he who should dispel wrong swings backwards and forwards?" The complaints are repetitive, and one wonders if the high steward was not worn down by his importunity rather than persuaded of the justice of his case. Here too the suffering has a human cause and the remedy is in human hands; the peasant is rewarded at public expense, and given the property of his oppressor in addition.

These several documents show no great depth of thought, but they show a concern with the problem of suffering.

6

One other addition will clarify the framework of these early speculations. This is the sense that conflict is somehow at the root of life. One or two examples will suffice.

In the Babylonian creation-myth, Tiamat, the Ocean, is the primeval goddess, together with Apsu, the power of sweet water. From them emerge by stages various other divine powers. There is conflict among these, as a result of which Apsu is killed. Tiamat now takes counter-measures, setting her son Kingu at the head of a host of monsters, scorpions, centaurs and the like. The great hero-god Marduk is appointed commander to resist the attack, and invested with sovereign authority. Armed with all the powers of the storm he advances on Tiamat and subdues her. Echoes of this conflict are heard in the *Psalms*, where Yahweh takes the place of Marduk:

> The floods have lifted up, O Lord,
>   the floods have lifted up their voice,
>   the floods lift up their roaring,
> Mightier than the thunders of many waters,
>   mightier than the waves of the sea,
>   the Lord on high is mighty.
>
> (*Ps.* 93, 3–4)

No doubt we have here a mythical picture of the sort of storm in which we tend automatically to say that "the elements are at war

with one another", combined with the fear of ocean-floods
natural to inhabitants of a river-delta. It may be that the historic
floods of Mesopotamia (represented in the famous legend of
Utnapishtim, the Mesopotamian Noah) were followed by unusual
encroachments from the sea, and that these were represented in
myth by the subduing of Apsu followed by the revenging of
Tiamat. However that may be, the priests and minstrels who
devised the story of a conflict between the gods were aware of a
conflict in their own minds, and a problem to be solved.

As a second example of conflict we may take the Ugaritic
myth, which we have already mentioned, of the conflict between
Baal and Mot. Baal and Mot seem in some ways to be doublets,
which would account for conflict between them. We have seen
how Baal refused to pay tribute to Mot, how Mot's threatening
words led Baal to humble submission, how none the less Baal
died, and how Anath mourned Baal and took revenge on Mot.
Finally, both gods seem to have been resurrected, and engage in a
fearful combat, fighting like wild animals and goring one another,
until there is eventually some kind of reconciliation. This myth
is much harder to interpret, but again we are bound to say that
those who devised it saw a conflict at the heart of things which
needed explanation.

In his remarkable study, *Python*, Fontenrose, starting from the
Greek myth of Apollo and the Dragon, has shown how widespread the theme of cosmic conflict is in the ancient world. He
instances from the Greek world, in addition to Apollo and Python,
Zeus and Typhon, Perseus and Medusa, Perseus and the sea-
monster, Heracles and Geryon, Heracles and the Hydra, and many
others. In all of these the adversary is a monster; in others he is
anthropomorphic. The Near East offers other and earlier versions
of the battle: among the Hittites, between the Weather God and
the dragon Illuyankas; in Mesopotamia, between the hero-god
Ninurta and the monster-demon Asag, or between Gilgamesh
and Humbaba; in Egypt, between Horus and Set, identified by
the Greeks with Typhon and often depicted as a hippopotamus.
Further away in India, Indra fights with the dragon Vritra.
Similar myths can be drawn from the Far East, from the Americas

and from Northern Europe. Furthermore, as Fontenrose has brilliantly shown, two familiar stories, Judith and Holofernes, and St. George and the dragon, are simply variants on the same theme. We have thus a widespread myth of conflict and combat, which is subsequently applied to ritual of different kinds: at Babylon to a New Year Festival; in Egypt again to rites of healing. Fontenrose's careful examination has shown that the myth comes before the ritual in these cases. What then does the myth express? Why is there conflict in the cosmos? Fontenrose eloquently concludes his great work (p. 474): "So we may look upon the whole combat in all its forms as the conflict between Eros and Thanatos. It is that opposition between life instincts and death instincts that Freud was the first to formulate, albeit tentatively, as the central principle of all living organisms from the beginning; though it was seen dimly and expressed in dramatic or metaphysical terms by poets and philosophers before him. But in life the two kinds of instincts, though opposed, are always mingled. Thus do the fantasies of myth disguise the fundamental truths of the human spirit."

The most familiar example of such conflict is in the Zoroastrian dualism of Persia. Zarathustra himself taught a sublime monotheism. Neither did the Amesha Spentas, the lieutenants of the Supreme God, receive worship, nor did he regard the power of evil as in any sense commensurate with the power of good. In the later developments of the Zendavesta we can, however, read the picture of the universe as split between the forces of good and evil, which are nicely balanced against one another. On the one side stands Ahura Mazda or Ormuzd, Lord of Light, and Author of all that is good; on the other stands Angra Mainyu or Ahriman, Lord of Darkness, and Author of all that is evil. The Children of Light confront the Children of Darkness all over the battlefield, which is the world. This is an antithesis of immeasurable influence. From Persia it spread to the Jews, and is found in the Dead Sea Scrolls. It also crept into Christianity, as in the book of *Revelation* where Satan has ceased to be one of the sons of God, as he appears in *Job*, and there is a cataclysmic conflict. The Christian writer will not allow an ultimate dualism, and the forces of Light are commanded not by the Supreme God but by Michael. How far there was an ultimate dualism in Zoroastrianism is uncertain. But no explanation of evil is given. It exists. Even in the Gathas, which represent more closely Zarathustra's own views, not only is the evil mind set against the good mind as a state of the individual, but the spirits which embody these attitudes are personified as Druj and Asha. There is thus a certain illogicality behind Zoroastrianism. On the one hand the Supreme God, the Power of Light and Good, is all in all. On the other, no explanation is given of evil, and in thought about human life it forms an existent power confronting the good. Or, to invert the comparison, on the one hand life is treated as a battleground between two forces, of good and evil, light and darkness, which are treated as "given", as ultimately existing; on the other, it is assumed that the good will win.

2

The Witness of the Greeks

1

The Homeric poems are our earliest written record of the mind of Greece, for the decipherment of Linear B, exciting though that is, has taken us little further than the material possessions of palaces and organization of kingdoms. In Homer there is a deep pessimism about human life. Greek and Trojans are alike described by adjectives meaning "wretched" or "miserable". The course of life is uncertain; the one thing that is certain is death.

> Of all that breathe and move on the face of the earth
> nowhere is to be found anything more miserable than man.
>
> *(Il.* 17, 446)

Two passages will suffice to illustrate, one from *The Iliad*, one from *The Odyssey*. In the first Achilles is addressing Priam, who has come to ransom Hector's body:

> Poor man, you have certainly had many evils to bear. . . .
> Come along, sit down on a chair, and we will let
> our griefs lie on our hearts, for all our sorrow;
> nothing is to be gained from moping and moaning.
> The gods have destined miserable mortals
> to live in sorrow, while they themselves know no cares.
>
> *(Il.* 24, 518 ff.)

In the other passage Odysseus has returned to Ithaca in a beggar's disguise, and one of the suitors has greeted him courteously. In his reply as a beggar he speaks of man in general:

Earth rears no feebler creature than man
of all that breathe and move on the face of the earth.
He thinks that he will never in the future face disaster,
so long as the gods give him success and his limbs move lightly.
But when the blessed gods add sorrow to his store,
that too he faces with a spirit of endurance, hard as he finds it.
Man's attitude to life on earth varies with the weather
the father of gods and men sends him.

(Od. 18, 130 ff.)

There is no exception and no redemption. Suffering is taken for
granted, not merely as a part, but as the dominant part of life.

Such was Homer's authority that this note recurs throughout
Greek poetry. Here is Hesiod (*WD* 101):

The land is full of evils, full of evils is the sea.

Here is Mimnermus (2):

We are as leaves which many-flowered spring
    gives birth to, when they grow in the sun's ra;sy
like them we joy in the flower of our youth
    for a short span, granted by the gods to know
no good, no ill. But at our side stand dark Death-spirits,
    one with a doom of burdensome age, one
with a doom of death. Briefly springs up the harvest
    of youth, as the sunlight spreads over the earth;
But when this season ends and passes, to be dead
    is better than life.
For many a sorrow seeds in the soul. Sometimes a house
    is wasted away and poverty's grim power prevails.
Or again a man is childless, and passes beneath the earth
    to death with that supreme yearning.
Or again disease grips and devours him. There's no man alive
    to whom Zeus does not bring sorrow on sorrow.

Here is Theognis (425):

For us on earth to be unborn is best
    and never to look on the beams of the shooting sun,
or, born, to reach Death's gates with all our speed
    and lie with earth piled high above.

Here is Pindar (*P.* 8, 95):

> Creatures of a day! What is a man? What is he not?
> A man is a dream of a shadow. . . .

2

The Greeks too know of gods who suffered; the rationalist J. M. Robertson called them "Pagan Christs". Martin Nilsson, probably the foremost scholar in this field, wrote in his *History of Greek Religion* (295): "The favourite idea of the age, the suffering of the god, was looked for in the ordinary agricultural labours. Thus the treading of the grapes in the winepress was interpreted as the dismembering of Dionysos, and the festival of the grape-harvest accordingly acquired a mystical Dionysiac character. An attempt seems to have been made to introduce the same idea into the corn-harvest, to judge by the verse: "When the young men cut off Demeter's limbs." Only Demeter and Dionysos afforded an opportunity for this idea, and hence the importance which the cults of these deities continued to possess."

In the legend of Demeter her child Persephone or Kore was seized by the king of the dead, Pluto or Hades, while she played with flowers in a meadow in Sicily—herself a fairer flower, said Milton. Demeter's grief was agonizing; she is the type of the *mater dolorosa*.

> She brought a bitter, cruel year for men
> over the fertile earth, and the land would not let
> its seed sprout; Demeter with her royal crown kept it hidden.
> In the fields oxen pulled many a curved plough to no purpose,
> many a grain of white barley fell idly on the earth.
>
> (Hom. *Hymn* 2, 305)

But Zeus had compassion. He commanded his brother of the underworld to release the girl, and reunited her to her mother. But she would spend a third of the year under the earth, and two-thirds in the light. Then Demeter relented, and the earth once again produced leaves, and flowers and fruit.

This beautiful story, here too concisely summarized, is an

aetiological myth. Demeter is the Earth-Mother or Corn-Mother. Persephone is the spirit of the seed-corn. Here the four bare months are not the months of winter but the bare bleak months of torrid summer, when the streams dry up, and everything is parched. During these months the seed-corn from the harvest was stored underground in large jars, waiting for the autumn rains and the autumn sowing. But although its origin is aetiological, its character goes far beyond the explanation of ritual. "The tale of Demeter and Persephone," wrote Michael Grant, "perhaps more than any other classical myth, has embodied and directed man's accumulated thoughts about being born and dying. It anticipates both Easter (in which life and death co-exist) and Christmas (the time of annual rebirth and hope)." The point here is threefold. First, the suffering of men is seen as part of cosmic suffering represented by the sorrowing of the Mother-goddess. Second, the pattern of life, of the very fertility of the earth, is seen as a texture of love and sorrow and joy. Third, in the Mysteries of Eleusis, men were permitted to share in the experience of new life. It is not too much to say that their sorrow was turned to joy.

> Blessed is the man on the face of the earth who has seen
> these mysteries; but the uninitiated who does not share in them,
> when dead, has a different destiny in darkness and gloom.
>
> (*Ib.* 480–2)

The mysteries have been well kept, but the story may have been acted out, and it seems that there was a moment when the worshippers cried to the sky "Rain!" and to the earth "Conceive!" and that the promise was revealed in the shape of an ear of corn.

Dionysus is much more of a puzzle. He seems like an intruder on the Greek scene, perhaps from Thrace or Asia Minor, and we have cataclysmic stories of the introduction of the worship. But Homer knew him well, though he did not allow him into the central group of the Olympians. Walter Otto conjectured long ago that Dionysus was more Hellenic than he appeared, and the appearance of the name in Linear B tablets may confirm this. He was perhaps a god of wild nature, nature in the raw. His women-worshippers would work themselves up into an ecstatic frenzy, roaming over the mountains in a whirling dance, and at the height of their "enthusiasm" would lay hands upon a wild animal and tear it limb from limb, devouring raw the bleeding flesh. In such acts the animal is commonly identified with the god, and the ritual is a ritual of communion; the worshipper becomes one with the god. Many stories are told of his presence driving people to madness, so that someone gets torn to pieces; the most familiar is the story of Pentheus, which is the theme of Euripides's play *The Bacchae*, as of Aeschylus's lost *Pentheus*. These may be legendary memories of those who tried to withstand his power; but it is at least possible that they represent original stories of the dismembering of the god himself, which have been rationalized and altered. In one story of the persecution of the god by Lycurgus, Dionysus is driven into the sea.

In the Orphic mysteries we find a myth, which we cannot directly attest before A.D. 200, though it must be centuries older, for Plato alludes to it. According to this myth Dionysus, the child of Zeus, won the hostile jealousy of the Titans, Zeus's traditional giant enemies. They distracted the child with toys, and seized, killed and ate him. Zeus consumed the criminals with a thunderbolt. From their ashes arose the race of men, who are thus a compound of the Titanic and the divine. Our aim must be to suppress the Titanic element in our nature, which is identified with the physical, and concentrate on developing the Dionysiac or spiritual element. This can be achieved through Orpheus and his mysteries, which make demands of ritual, ascetic and moral purity, and offer the chance of rebirth to eternal life. Meanwhile, Dionysus himself is the forerunner and exemplar of rebirth, for Athene rescued his heart, and from it Zeus caused Dionysus to be reborn, as Dionysus Zagreus, the god of the Orphic cult. Here again we have a pattern of death and rebirth to eternal life linked with the thought of a god who suffers.

3

Among the old stories of Greece was the legend of how king Agamemnon had led the Greek forces against Troy to avenge the rape of his brother's wife. The fleet was held back by contrary winds; in response to counsel from his religious adviser, Agamemnon sent for his own daughter and sacrificed her for a favourable wind. For ten years the army was away at Troy. Agamemnon's wife Clytemnestra took a lover, and when in the end Troy fell and Agamemnon returned, with a concubine of his own and with his daughter's blood still upon his hands, his wife trapped him in a bath and killed him. There remained a son of the marriage, Orestes, safe in another part of Greece, and a daughter, Electra. The boy grew to manhood. Duty, in days before police and law-courts, laid upon him the necessity of avenging his father by killing the assassin; to do this he had to kill his own mother.

With the origins of this legend we are not now concerned. It may represent in dramatic form the cycle by which the Old Year is killed by winter, and avenged by the New Year in turn. It may represent vividly primordial elements in the relation of man and woman, parent and child. It may even be a memory of actual historical occurrences, as the faithful Schliemann believed when he first dug at Mycenae. Our concern with it is that the first Athenian dramatist of genius took it as the theme of his greatest work, a connected series of three plays which we call *The Oresteia*, and which Swinburne described as the greatest spiritual work of man.

After *The Oresteia* Aeschylus wrote another trilogy on the theme of Prometheus, who defied the great god Zeus in order to be a benefactor of mankind. Unfortunately only the first of these three plays survives. In this we see the suffering of Prometheus, crucified on a mountain in the Caucasus for daring to help mankind in defiance of the edict of Zeus; we see the suffering of Io, a girl who has been the object of Zeus's infamous tyranny—for, as Gilbert Murray puts it, "the traditional tyrant in Greek poetry behaves like the traditional wicked baronet of the English stage". Finally, we learn that Prometheus has secret knowledge, and unless Zeus can secure this knowledge his power is doomed, and he will himself fall.

How did the drama end? We cannot be certain; we are in the

realm of speculation. But one thing we know. Out of the ordeal of suffering Io reached bliss and glory; she became the mother of the divine child Heracles. Furthermore, somehow Prometheus found release. In other words, in *The Prometheia* there is redemption from suffering. With Io it is not suggested that she has in any way merited the suffering she undergoes. Prometheus has in some sense chosen to suffer; he has acted in full knowledge of what the consequences will be. In the course of the drama he changes his purpose and decides to reveal the secret which he holds; but suffering he defies, and it cannot have been the suffering which produces the change. The change comes, we need not doubt, in response to a change in Zeus. There are signs elsewhere that Aeschylus attributes pity to the gods, and it may have been Io's unmerited suffering which called out pity from the supreme God. At any rate Zeus changes, and, in the most plausible interpretation, we can see the drama as a conflict between Power and Intelligence, in which "both have to concede something, and assimilate something, before they are reconciled in the later perfect cosmic order of Zeus". In some sense suffering is the background to that change.

"Do and suffer" is the assumption of *The Oresteia*; this is the essential, inexorable pattern of life—or so it seems. The wages of sin is death; they that take the sword shall perish by the sword; as we have done, so it shall be done to us. This is the decree of the Fates according to the ordination of Zeus. Here is the problem: once the cycle of death has started, it is unending; blood will have blood. But there is a clue to something deeper:

> Zeus, whose will has marked for man
> The sole way where wisdom lies;
> Ordered one eternal plan:
> Man must suffer to be wise.
> In visions of the night, like dropping rain,
> Descend the memories of pain—
> Man grows wise against his will.
> Stern is the grace, by Powers given
> Seated on the thrones of heaven.
>
> > (*Agamemnon* 186 ff. Tr. from various sources)

We must not make too much of this. One or two interpreters have tried to build upon this a theology, a theory that God too learns through suffering and the memories of pain. This is imagination running riot. What we have is a hint only; it is not worked out, and it is better that it should not be. We return to it in the last play of the series, when Orestes, pursued by the avenging Furies, speaks:

> Long schooled by pain, learned in cleansing ritual,
> I know when speech is lawful, when to hold my tongue.
>
>   *(Eumenides* 276–7)

The Furies too give the picture of life as they see it:

> Know that there is a throne which may not pass away,
> And one sits on it—Fear,
> Searching with steadfast eyes man's inner soul:
> Wisdom is child of pain, and born with many a tear.
>
>   *(Ibid.,* 517 ff.)

We act; we suffer; in memory, in dreams the pain returns; we learn; and, to put it at the lowest (for the last word in the drama is not with the Furies, and there are hints of a deeper meaning), fear redirects our steps. What follows shows us that Aeschylus is concerned primarily with the social implications of his theme. At the end of the drama, trial by jury replaces the blood-feud, the wheel of bloodshed is broken, and the terrible Furies are transformed into beneficent Earth-Goddesses. They themselves have already drawn out the social lesson. Immediately after the verse which asserts that Fear rules and Wisdom is the child of pain, they go on to sing:

> Seek neither licence, where no laws compel,
> Nor slavery beneath a tyrant's rod;
> Where liberty and rule are balanced well
> Success will follow as the gift of God.
>
>   *(Ibid.,* 526 ff.)

The full lesson of life cannot be learned under the arbitrary sway of despot or dictator, nor where anarchy prevails, but under the rule of law.

Suffering then is to Aeschylus in some sense a school of chastening. Dissatisfied with the idea of inherited guilt, he is groping
towards a deeper understanding than any which has gone before.
"His solution," writes Rose, "and it is characteristic of him, is
that the divine intent is not easy happiness for man, but hard-won
wisdom, which can be got only at the price of experience, often
of the bitterest kind. Why this should be the case, he does not
attempt to explain; it is the unsearchable will of the ruling power
. . . that it should be so, and Aeschylus' faith is robust enough to
trust the divine judgment, here as elsewhere."

4

Plato has been called *anima naturaliter Christiana*, "Moses speaking
Greek", "the only Greek who has attained the porch of truth"
(this last by Eusebius). The praise is extravagant, but it is at least a
counterweight to those moderns who revile him as a Nazi before
Hitler. In truth both are misleading. We shall not understand
Plato if we regard him as standing in a political situation other
than his own or representing a religion which he never knew.

Plato's thought was moulded by Socrates. This remarkable
man was born into the working-class; his father was a stone-
mason and his mother a midwife. He grew up with a keen interest
in the scientific thought of his day, but found himself increasingly
turning from the scientific question "How?" to the theological
question "Why?" This in turn directed his concentration from
the external world to man, from the macrocosm to the micro-
cosm, from physics and astronomy to ethics and politics. This is
what Cicero means when he says that Socrates brought Philosophy down from heaven and planted her on earth. Socrates's
mind, keen as Saladin's sword, sliced through conventional
religion and slipshod political thought, negative thinking and
hypocrisy. For most of the last part of his life Athens, an extreme
democracy, was at war with Sparta, an oligarchy. Socrates
criticized democracy on the grounds that politics require as much
expertise as any profession; an amateur piloting the ship of state
can do as much damage as an amateur piloting any other sort of

ship. His criticisms were absorbed by men like Alcibiades and Critias, who fancied themselves as the experts but who lacked the element of moral self-discipline which Socrates insisted on as the first quality of the true expert. The damage they did reflected on Socrates. In a time of political amnesty his political opinions could not be the object of direct attack. Instead he was prosecuted for religious unorthodoxy and mis-education. His defence was uncompromising, and he was condemned to death. In prison he had the opportunity of escaping. He refused, saying that he had accepted the protection of the laws when they favoured him and could not reject their verdict because it was unfavourable. He spent his last hours discussing the immortality of the soul with his friends, and, with a calmness that shamed them, drank the hemlock which was the Athenian method of execution, and died with the words to his closest friend: "Crito, we owe a cock to Asclepius." Asclepius was the god of healing; after life's fitful fever he slept well.

The pattern of Socrates's life and death left a deep impression upon his followers. More than once he had faced extreme danger rather than do wrong, for example when the left-wing mob, howling for the blood of military commanders who had failed to rescue the bodies of the fallen after a naval victory, demanded their mass-condemnation, an illegal motion which Socrates from the chair refused to put, or when the right-wing dictator tried to implicate him in the process of unjust arrest and condemnation and he turned on his heel and walked away. In the end he had died for his principles. This pattern finds expression in Plato in the conviction that "it is worse to commit injustice than to suffer injustice". We must be loyal to the good, even though that loyalty bring danger and death. This is a doctrine of the *irrelevance* of suffering. In its simplest terms, Plato's answer to the problems "Why should the righteous suffer?" and "Why should the wicked flourish?" is "If the end of life is virtue, why think that it has anything to do with prosperity? If it is prosperity, why think that it has anything to do with virtue?" Man is compounded of soul and body, but it is his soul which is his immortal part; it is his soul that really matters. Pain and disease touch the body; they do not touch the soul. Wrongdoing affects the soul, the self, the personality. What the body absorbs is soon gone. What the soul absorbs is with you always; for good or bad, you can, and do, take it with you. So Socrates defended himself: "I spend all my time going round trying to persuade you, whatever your age, to put first the supreme welfare of your souls, not your bodies or possessions. . . . If this doctrine corrupts the young, then I would have to plead guilty." The corollary of this is the survival of the soul, and in *Phaedo* Plato argues for this with an eloquence seldom surpassed, and in several of his works depicts mythically the soul's ultimate destiny.

Alongside this Plato teaches the chastening effect of suffering as a corrective. Hence his paradox that the greatest disaster which can occur to a man is to do wrong and escape punishment, a view which he maintains against the immoralists who claim that to do wrong and get away with it is the height of beatitude. There is, Plato claims, a parallel between medical science and penology: the one aims at restoring physical health, the other moral health. The patient whose disease is recognized and treated is better off than the man who is ill but refuses to acknowledge the fact and rejects all treatment. The delinquent whose moral abnormality is recognized and treated by punishment is better off than the delinquent who escapes punishment. There is then a form of suffering, administered in punishment, which is *remedial*, which "brings the offender into tune again". It is interesting to recall that the word "pain" is derived from the Latin *poena*, "punishment". Plato's pupil Aristotle describes punishment as a kind of allopathy, which cures an excessive inclination to pleasure by a dose of pain.

Yet with all this there are glimpses that Plato was groping towards something deeper. It is not only that suffering, which is beneficial to the wrongdoer, is irrelevant to the man of righteousness, but that it is almost expected of him. There is something in Plato which drew from the Christian commentator the words, "Plato gives, in several passages of his writings, a description of a just man suffering, which corresponds, almost line for line, with the picture which the Gospels draw of the persecution and condemnation of the Saviour; even the blow on the cheek, which the noble Sufferer had to endure from the rude soldiers, is not forgotten." This is not unjustified; the coincidences are surprising. In his greatest work, *The Republic*, Plato depicts mankind as prisoners chained in a cave facing one direction. Behind them is a parapet, and beyond the parapet a path along which people walk with images, models and puppets on their heads. Beyond this a fire blazes, so that the shadows of the images are thrown on the wall of the cave before the prisoners' eyes. These shadows are all the prisoners have ever seen; they are the only reality they know. If one of them is released and taken out into the sunlight, he will at first be blinded by the brilliance, but as his eyes become acclimatized he will learn to perceive, first shadows, then objects, and finally the Sun which is the source of sight and light. This is the man who has glimpsed the reality, the lover of wisdom, the philosopher. If now he returns to the cave he will be blinded by the darkness and unable to recognize the shadows. The prisoners will say that he has lost his sight. They will scorn him; mock him, persecute him, kill him. *None the less, go back he must.*

Plato does not explain this assertion; he does not elaborate it or justify it; but it is hard not to see in it some kind of embryonic outline of a redemptive doctrine of suffering.

5

The word "Cynic" has changed its meaning. It is derived from the Greek word for "dog", which was the nickname of Diogenes, the founder of the sect. The Cynics were the Dogged Philosophers; they lived freely like dogs, were the watchdogs of true values, and growled at wrong-doers. They were the extreme nonconformists of the ancient world, attacking convention, putting false ideas out of circulation as ruthlessly as a bank official would deal with dud coins, and practising a radical form of nonattachment. This led them to an abandonment of local ties, and its corollary of cosmopolitanism. "Where do you come from?" "Everywhere." "What do you mean?" "I am a citizen of the universe." It led them to abandon property and to espouse my lady Poverty. Diogenes reduced his possessions to a scrip, a staff, and a large earthenware jar for shelter. It led them to measures of ascetic discipline, rolling naked in the torrid sand and in the heat of a summer's noon, or embracing a marble statue in the snow through the cold of a summer's night. Such an approach to life might, and did, encourage a fraudulent mendicancy. It might, and did, tempt even its finer adherents to shock merely for the sake of shocking. But it also offered an important critique of society, and produced men, like Diogenes himself, or Crates and his wonderful wife Hipparchia, of great nobility of character.

Among the Cynics there emerged a doctrine of suffering. It is associated first with the figure of Heracles (whom the Romans called Hercules), the type of the Cynic saint. His twelve labours were allegorically interpreted, and the word "labour" became a technical term of Cynic preachers. His cleansing of the Augean stables was an example of humble service; it was an assault on the popular view that great men do not stoop to menial tasks, on the conventional distaste of the privileged for mucky jobs. He went through solitariness, nakedness, poverty, homelessness and suffering—and through this was the son of the Most High, ruler of earth and sea, and fitted because of his labours to be admitted among the number of the gods.

A second Cynic model was Odysseus:

> Sing in me, Muse, and through me tell the story
> of that man skilled in all ways of contending,
> the wanderer, harried for years on end.

Odysseus is the man who is restored to his kingdom through and after years of suffering. The motif dates back to Antisthenes, an associate of Socrates and precursor of the Cynics. To him Odysseus is the resourceful individualist, whose aim is the service of others, and whose method includes voluntary suffering and self-abasement. Later Odysseus's homecoming provides an analogy for the Cynic saint—the true king in the clothes of a slave, alone and defenceless, suffering abuse and insult from the drunken arrogance of those who think that they hold power.

A third model was Socrates, who lived in poverty, suffered abuse, and died the death of a criminal.

The most illuminating passages showing the attitude of the Cynics to suffering are found in two speeches by Dio Chrysostom —the nickname means "golden-mouthed". Dio was born at Prusa in Bithynia about A.D. 40, trained in the skill of public oratory, and converted to philosophy by Musonius Rufus, a Stoic with Cynic leanings. His outspoken criticisms of the emperor Domitian won him disfavour, and from 82 to 96 he was in exile, living the life of an itinerant preacher. In the eighth speech, given during his exile, perhaps at some athletic gathering, he tells a story of Diogenes attending an athletic contest. "Have you come as a spectator?" someone asked. "No," he replied, "to take part." This provoked laughter. "Who against?" "The toughest opponents imaginable—hardships." And now I quote *verbatim*: "The man of nobility reckons hardships his greatest antagonists. He is for ever contesting with them, night and day, not for a sprig of parsley (goats do that!) or a spray of olive or pine, but for happiness and virtue throughout his life. . . . He is not afraid of his opponents, he doesn't pay to draw someone different. He challenges them all, round by round, grappling with hunger and cold, standing up to thirst, disclosing no weakness even if he has to survive the whip, the fire and the knife. Hunger, exile and loss of reputation hold no terrors for him. They are all trivialities. The full-grown man in their grip often laughs like boys with knuckle-bones and coloured balls." The next speech is closely similar. In this Diogenes appears with a pine-wreath. The authorities ask him to take it off on the grounds that he has won no victory. This gives him the opening he is waiting for. "On the contrary I have beaten many formidable opponents, not like these slaves here, wrestling and running and throwing the discus"—the Cynics called slaves all who were still subject to their passions—"but far more difficult opponents, poverty, exile, ill-repute, yes, and anger, pain, desire, fear, and that most redoubtable beast of all, treacherous and cowardly, pleasure." The catalogue of sufferings has an interesting comparison with that of Paul.

In the Cynic attitude to suffering it is possible to trace four elements. The first arises from a pessimistic outlook on life, which tells us something of the mood of the times in which Cynicism grew and flourished. It is an attitude which is well expressed by A. E. Housman:

> Therefore, since the world has still
> Much good, but much less good than ill,
> And while the sun and moon endure
> Luck's a chance, but trouble's sure,
> I'd face it as a wise man would,
> And train for ill and not for good.

Secondly, and alongside this, there is the attitude which sees the wise man or saint as in a minority, and inevitably despised and rejected of men. He is the king surrounded by slaves, but he is unrecognized. Odysseus in rags in his own palace is here the type, and the comparison with Diogenes is explicitly made, though Diogenes is said to surpass Odysseus in patience. There is here an element of arrogance which mars the Cynic standpoint; the Cynic preacher does tend to see himself as saved and the rest as damned, and he has not even the Calvinistic virtue of attributing that salvation to the inscrutable power of the Almighty; it is the product of his own will. Thirdly, there is an element of masochism in the Cynic make-up; no one who was not something of a masochist would embrace the Cynic way of life, and it is clear that, Crates and Hipparchia apart, the leading Cynics did not experience normal sexual fulfilment. Fourthly, and finally, there is a groping sense that suffering has somehow been written into the scheme of things and it is *right* to undergo suffering. This is not worked out; it is not even unambiguously expressed, but it does less than justice to the Cynics to suppose that it is not there.

6

The Stoics sometimes seem like a group of Cynics who have been accepted into the Establishment and have toned down all that might give offence. Certainly Zeno, the founder of the "Porch", was much influenced by Diogenes; they said that he wrote his early *Republic* "under the Dog's tail". Certainly also in a man like Epictetus the strands are impossible to disentangle. But the two schools were distinct and remained distinct.

The Stoics are important for their thorough-going pantheism. In this their outlook is close to that of the Hindus. Here is the voice of Seneca: "We understand Jupiter to be ruler and guardian of the whole, the mind and life-force of the universe, the lord and artificer of this fabric. Every name is his. Would you call him fate? You will not err. He it is upon whom all things depend, the cause of causes. Would you call him Providence? You will be right. He it is whose thought provides for the universe that it may move on its course unhurt and do its part. Would you call him Nature? You will not be speaking falsely. He it is of whom all things are born, by whose life-force we live. Would you call him Universe? You will not be deceived. He himself is this whole that you see, fills his own parts, sustains himself and what is his" (QN. 2, 45). If God is all and in all, then, in the cliché, all must be for the best in the best of all possible worlds. If suffering is not an illusion, the attitude which regards suffering as evil, undesirable and to be avoided must be a delusion. For, according to the Stoic view, the suffering which we experience is a part of the very being of God; it must be right, it must be for the best. The Stoic view found its clearest expression in an unexpected quarter, centuries later, the Roman Catholic Alexander Pope's *Essay on Man*:

> All are but parts of one stupendous whole,
> Whose body, Nature is, and God the soul;
> That, chang'd thro' all, and yet in all the same,
> Great is the earth, as in th' aetherial frame,
> Warms in the sun, refreshes in the breeze,
> Glows in the stars, and blossoms in the trees,
> Lives thro' all life, extends thro' all extent,
> Spreads undivided, operates unspent,
> Breathes in our soul, informs our mortal part,
> As full, as perfect, in a hair as heart;
> As full, as perfect, in vile Man that mourns,
> As the rapt Seraph that adores and burns;

To him no high, no low, no great, no small;
He fills, he bounds, connects and equals all.
   Cease then, nor ORDER Imperfection name:
Our proper bliss depends on what we blame.
Know thy own point: This kind, this due degree
Of blindness, weakness, Heav'n bestows on thee.
Submit—In this, or any other sphere,
Secure to be as blest as thou canst bear:
Safe in the hand of one disposing Pow'r,
Or in the natal, or the mortal hour.
All Nature is but Art, unknown to thee;
All Chance, Direction, which thou canst not see;
All Discord, Harmony, not understood;
All partial Evil, universal Good;
And, spite of Pride, in erring Reason's spite,
One truth is clear, "Whatever IS, is RIGHT".

(1, 267 ff.)

So Cleanthes (whom Pope doubtless had in mind) in his *Hymn to Zeus*:

Ah! but thou knowest to make crooked straight,
order in chaos, and love where no love is,
So hast thou fitted all evil with all good,
to make both one, in one eternal Principle.

Epictetus was a Stoic, something of a saint, and a great teacher; he was also a slave and a cripple. He asserts a complete unity and harmony for the cosmos. If Zeus does not ensure that his own citizens are as happy as he, there is something wrong. Is he not then to grumble at his slavery? "What does Zeus say? 'Epictetus, if it had been possible, I would have made your little body and your little property free. . . . Since I was not able to do this, I have given you a little portion of myself.'" But this is no answer. Compensation may balance a wrong, but it does not annul it, and the characteristic diminutives soften the problem without removing it. What about his lameness? "Must my leg then be blamed? Slave! [a technical Stoic term opposed to the philosopher-king] do you then find fault with the universe for one wretched leg? Will you not willingly surrender it for the whole." All partial Evil, universal Good. But if the lameness of his leg is necessary to the well-being of the universe, he may legitimately ask why; and if not, it does not really help to say, "So much is right; why grumble at one leg?" because to theology a slight imperfection is as great a problem as a great one (as the Stoics with their ethical paradoxes ought to have seen), and because it is his leg in a way in which it is not his universe.

7

The Epicureans add one factor of some importance. Like the Stoics they were the product of a new age in which leisure for education went with political impotence and a general sense of instability and insecurity. Like all the philosophies of the Hellenistic Age, Epicureanism made a virtue of *autarcy*, self-sufficiency, that which Aldous Huxley calls non-attachment. Epicurus called the Cynics "the enemies of Greece", but in this he is close to them: "We regard autarcy as a great good, not with a view to always making do with a little, but to finding a little sufficient if we have not got a lot, frankly realizing that it is the people who least need luxury who enjoy it most, and that only bagatelles are hard to come by, whereas that which is natural is easy to procure. Plain fare gives as much pleasure as an expensive menu, when once the pain of want has been removed. Bread and water offer the keenest pleasure when a hungry man tackles them. So to accustom oneself to a simple, inexpensive régime provides all that is needful for health, and enables a man to face more readily the inescapable demands of life. It places us in a better position when we do occasionally come upon luxuries. It enables us to face fortune fearlessly" (DL 10, 130–1). The Epicureans were not the crude pleasure-seekers which ancient and modern slanders have made them out to be. It was Epicurus who said that the wise man would be happy even on the rack (DL 10, 118). The key-word for Epicureans was *ataraxia*, which means "freedom from being shaken", "tranquillity".

But at two points Epicurus went beyond the apparent logic of autarcy. The first, which does not concern us here, was in the

stress placed upon friendship. Epicurus criticized Stilpo for suggesting that the wise man, being "non-attached", did not need
friends, and in a remarkable dictum declared: "Friendship goes
dancing round the world proclaiming to us all to awake to the
praises of the happy life" (*Gn. V.* 52). He rationalized this by
deriving it from what Kropotkin was to call Mutual Aid, but, this
done, declared that friendship should always be pursued for its
own sake (23).

The second point concerned pity. Most of the apostles of
autarcy banished pity; for if we show pity, our peace of mind
depends on circumstances outside our control. Even before the
Hellenistic Age set in, Aristotle had suggested that pity, like fear,
was an undesirable effect to be purged from our system by regular
doses of tragic drama (*Poet.* 1449 b 27). Zeno declared that pity
is a sickness of the soul, which no one would display but a frivolous
fool (Cic. *Mur.* 29, 61). Seneca suggests that we should act help-
fully, but that to show pity is to show a weak character: "It is
only weak eyes which weep in sympathy" (*Clem.* 2, 5, 1). Epictetus tells his hearers: "You must feel no anger, no rage, no envy,
no pity" (3, 24, 2). Even Plotinus, with his towering mystical
vision of God, said: "It is weakness to be touched with any feeling
of pity for misery" (1, 4, 8). It might be expected that Epicurus,
with his stress on tranquillity, would sound this note louder than
others; on the contrary he actually advocates pity (e.g. D.L. 10,
118). He does not justify this philosophically. The fact remains that
to Epicurus we cannot attain tranquillity of mind unless we are
prepared to weep with those who weep and suffer with those who
suffer. There is pain and pleasure in the universe; this is a fact of
life which Epicurus does not try to explain. The aim of life is at
each point to secure a maximum excess of pleasure over pain or a
minimum excess of pain over pleasure. We do not attain this by
plunging thoughtlessly into pleasures or running blindly away
from pain. At a deeper level, suffering is not incompatible with
happiness. Through the acceptance of suffering we may find
happiness.

3
The Witness of the Romans

1

The Roman tradition was not reflective and philosophical.

> Others will hammer more passion out of steaming bronze—
> I am quite sure—will draw living features out of marble,
> will be better at presenting cases, will outline with compass
> the paths of the sky, will record the risings of the stars:
> Man of Rome, be sure to use your authority for government—
> that's where your science is going to be—habituate men to peace,
> show mercy to those who submit, and war down the proud.
>
> (Vergil *Aen.* 6, 842 ff.)

We shall not expect much theoretical exploration of the place of suffering in life. But there is a practical acceptance which is seen in the character the Romans admired. This character is summed up in the single word *virtus*. *Virtus* does not mean "virtue", at least not till the Ilissus had overflowed its banks into the Tiber. *Virtus* is "being a man" where a man is the head of his house, with absolute authority to be exercised without sentimentality, even to life and death; he is a farmer in mountainous country; he is a citizen, and to be a citizen in face of hostile tribes meant to be a soldier. So *virtus* appears in school-vocabularies as "courage"; this is almost as misleading as the rendering "virtue". *Virtus* means "toughness"; males have it as opposed to females; adults have it as opposed to children; real men have it as opposed to cowards and weaklings. It means a capacity for hard work in all weathers, and an ability to protect your family, and the extended family which is the state, against wild animals, bandits and foreign raiders. Caesar says that the Helvetii are superior to the rest of the Gauls in toughness, *virtus*, because they spend all their time fighting with the Germans (*BG* 1, 1). Cicero, seeking to place Rome in the stream of Greek philosophy, but deeply imbued with the traditions of Rome, says that *virtus* has in his day taken on a broader meaning, but it should be properly confined to the capacity to scorn death and bear pain (*TD* 2, 18, 43).

The type of character the Romans admired may be seen in Lucius Junius Brutus, founder of the Roman Republic, who when his sons offended against the law, unflinchingly ordered their execution. To understand what this meant we must project ourselves back to a situation where family ties were far more potent than they are over most of the world today and where there was an almost pathological insistence on sons for the succession. Or we may instance T. Quinctius Cincinnatus, who was found by the nation's representatives working on his farm, appointed dictator with plenary power in a crisis, won a notable military victory over the Aequi, and within sixteen days had resigned his office and was back on the farm again. It matters little whether the anecdotes were based on fact, though there are no real grounds for the scepticism of some modern critics. What matters is the quality of toughness which the Romans admired. This is the centre of what Ennius meant by his celebrated *moribus antiquis res stat Romana virisque*: "The prosperity of Rome depends upon the traditional Roman character and the toughness of the Romans." Haarhoff has compared the Romans in this with the Voortrekkers.

Another example is illuminating. This is M. Atilius Regulus, general in Africa during the first war against Carthage. He was not endowed with the more obviously desirable qualities; he was vain and incompetent, and through his ambition to win the war himself involved his country in disastrous defeat. Yet Cicero takes him again and again as the type of *virtus*. Why? Because history, or legend, or a mixture of both told how Regulus was sent to Rome on parole to return if the Carthaginian prisoners held by the Romans were not released, and how Regulus went to Rome and advised the senate not to release the prisoners, who were worth more to Rome than he was, and how he then kept his sworn word and returned fearlessly to a cruel death.

D

No more a citizen, they tell that he
pushed from him his wife's embrace, his young
 children, and sternly fixed
  his tough gaze on the ground
till his words impressed the wavering senate
with advice never heard before or since,
 and with his friends in tears
  he chose a noble disgrace.
He knew what the cruel executioner
had ready for him; yet he pushed aside
 family standing in his path,
  crowds checking his departure,
just as if he'd finished a protracted case
for a client now that judgment had been delivered
 and was making for Venafrum's fields
  or Spartan Tarentum.

        (Hor. *Od.* 3, 5, 41 ff.)

So Horace tells the story. Whatever Regulus had done, he was prepared to suffer; what seemed admirable in him was partly the ultimate patriotism and partly the impassive toughness of the man.

 Horace in another of the six great Roman odes sketches the character the Romans admired.

When a man's upright and grips his wheel stoutly
his resolution's firm, he can't be shaken
 by mob-violence, or by the glare
  of a threatening dictator, or by
the gale, storming king of the uneasy Adriatic,
or by the thunder-god hurling his lightning.
 If the world collapses in pieces,
  its fall will find him unafraid.

        (3, 3, 1 ff.)

The point in all these passages is that the world is hostile. We must expect trials and tribulations. The best man is the man who shows toughness of personality in a world like that.

2

One Roman looked deeper. This was Vergil. In his younger days he was, as Horace had been, an Epicurean, partly out of a naturally retiring and gentle temperament, partly out of philosophical conviction. This is important in two ways. First, the Epicureans believed that the original state of man was a violent and poverty-stricken barbarism, and his life, as Thomas Hobbes put it, solitary, poor, nasty, brutish and short, but that man could rise and had risen above such a state. Secondly, as we have seen, the Epicureans were rare among ancient thinkers in making a virtue out of compassion, which Aristotle and the Stoics accounted a vice, because to be compassionate is to place your peace of mind at the mercy of circumstances beyond your control. Compassion shines from Vergil's poetry, whether it be compassion for an ox who has lost his partner (G 3, 518) or for a mother who has lost her son (A 9, 473 ff.), or a subtle self-identification with Dido and Turnus. Even when he is depicting Aeneas as a Stoic sage, who has, so to speak, "passed the test" and "arrived", he allows his Epicurean humanity to get the better of him, and permits Aeneas to show pity, pity for the unburied dead, which actually induces him to criticize the government of the universe (A 6, 332), and pity for Lausus in the very act of killing him (10, 821-4). Many critics have seen Vergil's philosophy as summed up in three words from *The Aeneid*—*sunt lacrimae rerum* (1, 462). Much ink and ingenuity have been spilled on the interpretation of these words. Is the genitive subjective or objective? Do the words mean "The very stones weep" or "We weep even over the stones"? Or is it more general? Is the meaning "There are tears at the heart of the universe", and, if so, once again, is it the universe which weeps, or we who weep for it? The question is misguided. For the Latin words not merely can but do mean all of these things; to differentiate is a process of analysis called out by translation into another tongue. Vergil's compassion is comprehensive; it arises from the ground of all being and embraces the universe.

Vergil no doubt began to reflect on the problem of suffering with the ruthless slaughter and evictions of the civil wars. But it is only in *The Georgics* that we can trace his mature judgment. Dryden called *The Georgics* "the best poem of the best poet", and this maturity of judgment is an element in its greatness. The countryside of *The Eclogues* is an idealized Arcadia; they are mimes or playlets. In *The Georgics* we are dealing with the real thing; it has been called a hymn to *labor improbus*. For the farmers of *The Georgics* are no absentee gentlemen-farmers; they are the people who do the work. They have to be hardy (1, 160) as the work they do is hard (2, 412); but mankind is a hardy breed (1, 63). The work is never done (2, 397–401). Without the effort of men everything is destined to slide downhill, like a rowing-boat in a swift current, if the oarsman once stops rowing (1, 197 ff.). We note how many of the words Vergil uses to describe ordinary agricultural operations imply effort (e.g. 1, 99; 145; 220), or how he piles up hints of jobs to be done, or offers the epigrammatic advice, "Admire large estates; farm a small one" (2, 412). This is the point from which Theodor Haecker starts his appreciation of *The Georgics*, stressing Vergil's "complete understanding of the essential nature of toil".

If this were all, *The Georgics* would be a pessimistic poem. But it is not. For Vergil sees the labour of the farmer as arising from the deliberate policy of Jupiter:

> The Father of farming
> did not want the way to be easy. He was the first to use science
> to turn the sod, sharpening men's minds on the whetstone of
>   difficulties,
> not letting his realms slumber in unstirring sloth.
>
> (1, 121 ff.)

It was Jupiter who made snakes poisonous, commanded wolves to plunder, deprived man of fire and put an end to the Golden Age as a challenge to man to develop science for himself. It is by destiny, by Jupiter's proclaimed law, that everything worsens unless man's efforts improve it. The analysis of social evolution is Epicurean, but Vergil has come to put it in the context of divine purpose. Life is hard; but life always had been hard, unless in some mythical Golden Age. Hard work is unpleasant but hard work, however unpleasant, combined with the pressure of poverty, wins every battle (1, 145). The end is good; we see the fields laughing and bountiful, and this—the single Latin word *laetus* covers both thoughts—is one of the most characteristic of Vergil's adjectives in *The Georgics*; in the poem's first four words he says that his purpose is to tell "what makes the crops laughing-and-bountiful". In other words Vergil, scrutinizing man's encounter with Nature, came to the conclusion that behind the universe lay a power that was intelligible, not unfriendly, and justified in its underlying purposes. Tenney Frank wrote of Vergil: "It is in the contemplation of a life of toil that he finds his honest philosophy of life: the gospel of salvation through work. Hardships whet the ingenuity of man: God himself for man's own good brought an end to the age of golden indolence, shook the honey from the trees and gave vipers their venom. Man has been left alone to contend with an obstinate nature, and in that struggle to discover his own world." Difficulties are there by divine dispensation as a spur to man's efforts. They are there to overcome.

The theme of *The Georgics* might be described as "Through labour to prosperity", the theme of *The Aeneid* as "Through suffering to empire". The theme is sounded near the beginning of the poem, when Aeneas says to his men: *O passi graviora, dabit deus his quoque finem*, "You have suffered worse than this; God will bring this to an end too." Aeneas faces three tests, just as the hardships of Nature test the farmer. The first is the loss of his country and his wife. This test he fails. His behaviour is irrational:

> I snatched up my arms without thinking; arms offered nothing to
> a man of sense,
> but my fervour yearned to pile into the battle, and to speed to the
> citadel
> with allies at my side. Half-crazed and furious I made my decisions
> hastily.
>
> (2, 314 ff.)

Again, when he finds Creusa gone, his behaviour, however

loving, is again irrational, and endangers his whole destiny and
the rest of his family's safety. The second test is the temptation of
Dido's love. Again his behaviour is irrational; he forgets his
destiny for his passion, and has to be recalled by a divine mes-
senger. It is not only our romanticism which sides with Dido.
Aeneas himself does; he sheds tears at her pleas, but is unshaken
in his renewed resolve to fulfil his destiny, as an oak-tree may shed
its leaves before a gale, but remain unshaken (4, 437 ff.). For the
path to empire is paved with suffering, and Aeneas has inevitably
intensified that suffering by his original distraction; life would be
meaningless if our sins made no difference. The third test is the
burning of the boats in Sicily. This time Aeneas all but forgets his
destiny (5, 704), but the words of an old sailor named Nautes
recall him:

> Son of Venus, Destiny drags us this way and that; let us follow.
> Come what come may, if we face fortune we can climb on top of
> it.

This is his last test. He has now been "tried in the fire of destiny"
(5, 725). There is much suffering to come. Palinurus will lie on an
unfamiliar sandbank, Euryalus will be cut down, like a flower by
a plough, Pallas and Lausus and Camilla and Turnus will perish
and pity will not save them. But this is destiny, and destiny, *fatum*,
is the keynote of *The Aeneid*. Vergil is not of course merely
telling the epic of Aeneas. All that he writes foreshadows the
destiny of Rome, and when Dido cries

> Arise, some avenger from my bones,
> to harry the Trojan settlers with fire and sword,
> now, in the future, whenever strength is granted.
> Set shore against shore, wave against wave,
> I implore, army against army. Let them fight, and their children's
> children.
>
> (4, 623 ff.)

she is reminding the Roman reader of the terrible war against
Hannibal, who occupied Italy for three times as long as the Nazis
occupied France—yes, and the danger from Cleopatra too. For it
is historically true that Rome reached power through her resilience

in defeat. And when Vergil ventured to bring the royal family to tears by his prophecy of the death of young Marcellus (6, 882 ff.) he did so in the knowledge that he was presenting a view of life which is not so different from William Penn's *No Cross, No Crown*.

For Vergil's later writings do offer a philosophy of suffering. Reduced to a coldly prosaic analysis it amounts to three propositions. First, hardship is deliberately written into the scheme of things by the God who controls our destinies. Second, its object is to test and challenge us to greater things. Third, if we accept our destiny, face the challenge and surmount the test, we shall win through. It is interesting to notice how close this is to Toynbee's philosophy of history, that civilizations emerge in response to a challenge that is sufficient but not excessive, and that without such a challenge there is no progress.

3

One further feature of Roman society under the Empire is here relevant; it might be called almost an extension of Vergil's philosophy of life. This has to do with the worship accorded to emperors. It is not necessary here to go into all the precedents which Augustus had before him, from the divine Pharaohs of Egypt to the Greek cults of city-founders. The most important immediate precedent was provided by Cicero in *Scipio's Dream* when he wrote (3, 1): "All who have saved, succoured, or glorified their country have a sure allotted place in heaven, where these blessed souls will enjoy everlasting life. Nothing on earth is more acceptable to the supreme God who rules the universe than the counsels and societies of states, that is, of men lawfully gathered together. Their rulers and preservers proceed from Heaven and to Heaven they return." This doctrine of Cicero's relates immortality to mortal achievement, and makes divinity the reward of service. The picture emerged of Olympus as a heavenly replica of the Roman senate, with some who sat by right, and others co-opted for services rendered.

The legendary prototype of such service was provided by

Heracles-Hercules. He was the son of Zeus, but that did not auto-matically give him divinity; Zeus had many such children. It has in fact been argued that he was a historical baron of Tiryns who combined temper, gluttony and lust with toughness, generosity and enterprise. At any rate to subsequent generations he was the man who had imposed on him, and successfully fulfilled, twelve labours, and in the end for his labours and service of others was welcomed into heaven and married to Hebe. In the original legend the power of adventurous endurance is more prominent than the element of service. But the legend was worked over by preachers, and Prodicus preached a celebrated sermon telling how Heracles was confronted with two women, one of easy beauty, and easy virtue, named Pleasure, and the other of severer but more lasting beauty, called Duty, and eschewed the former and espoused the latter. Later Stoics and Cynics, as we have seen, took Heracles, slightly oddly, as the pattern of the ideal sage.

Alexander the Great used to appear in public with the club and lionskin of Heracles (Ath. 12, 537); this was no doubt in confirma-tion of his claim to be the son of Zeus Ammon, rather than in any special desire to appear as a benefactor; incidentally, he claimed Heracles as his ancestor. Among his successors the urge to be known as benefactor was so strong that it became an imperial title—Euergetes—and Jesus in his day mocked at it. Julius Caesar, who claimed his descent from the goddess Venus, used the claim of divine origin as the basis of a claim to divinity, as his coins show in the midst of somewhat conflicting literary evidence, and with the appearance of a comet in the July after his murder he was firmly established in heaven as the divine Julius. Augustus, who in face of Caesar's murder and Antony's claim to be an Oriental divine monarch, Dionysus-Osiris incarnate, consort of Cleopatra-Isis, queen of Egypt, had to move with caution, felt able to style himself *divi filius*, son of the divine one, referring to his adoptive father Julius. This did not of itself imply divinization, but it put his foot on the ladder; it placed him in the same category as Heracles and Asclepius, who being the sons of gods were, so to speak, candidates for divinity, and by their service to mankind passed the entrance examination. Tiberius made the comparison explicitly in his speech at Augustine's funeral when he drew the parallel with Heracles (D.C. 56, 56), and in a rescript based the divinity of Augustus on "the magnitude of his benefactions to the whole world". In this same rescript he called Augustus his father; he had of course been adopted as heir, but the phrase set his own foot on the ladder. His good sense asserted his own mortality and humanity (T. *Ann.* 4, 38), but at one moment the comparison with Heracles burst out. Tiberius did not suffer gladly fools and flatterers, and he had the type of wit which hurts more than it heals. A courtier spoke to him of his "holy responsibilities". "Not holy," snapped Tiberius; "laborious." It was a sane rebuke to sycophancy; it also put him in the category of Heracles, who after death was divinized for his labours. By the Flavian period in the latter part of the first century, it was established that only a megalomaniac such as Caligula and Nero had shown themselves, and Domitian proved to be, would assert his own divinity and demand his worship during his lifetime, but that a good emperor might expect to attain divinity on his death, and the blunt soldier Vespasian, conscious that he had restored Rome from the very brink of disaster, remarked, as he felt death approach, "Oh dear, I think I'm becoming a god!"

It is not needful to pursue the theme further. What has happened is that Vergil's outlook has burst the confines of literary fiction into the highest flights of politics. The powers behind the world have so ordered things that it is only by rejecting a life of ease and accepting a life of laborious service that we can fulfil ourselves and our destinies. It is the combination of divine birth and tough, selfless, laborious service that sets a man in heaven.

4

The Witness of the Jews

We must now move back somewhat in time to see how the Hebrews faced the problem of suffering, which has been seared so deeply into their life. The key moment to the understanding of Hebrew religion is the Exodus from Egypt. There, at the great moment of their deliverance, they entered into a solemn covenant with Yahweh, the mountain-god of the Kenites, who was associated with the volcano Sinai. Two aspects of this covenant made it one of the key-moments of history. First, it was free. Yahweh was not a tribal god in the same way that Chemosh of Moab was a tribal god. If Moab were wiped out, Chemosh ceased to exist. With Yahweh it was not so. Israel might depend on him; he did not depend on them. This made for the transformation of Yahweh from a tribal god to the one god of the whole world. Monolatry, the worship of one god out of many, gave way to monotheism, the belief in one god only. When one tribe met another in battle, in normal belief it was a conflict of gods, and the god of the weaker tribe was himself defeated. But to the Israelites any defeat they suffered was due to the displeasure of Yahweh. Further, as he became the universal god, so his power was absolute. Everything was done by his will. The author of *Exodus* says time and again, in words which caused much trouble to Christian theologians later, "The Lord hardened the heart of Pharaoh" (9.12; cf. 4.21; 7.13; 10.1; 10.20; 10.27; 11.10; 14.4; 14.8, etc.). If God is responsible for everything, then everything must be explained according to his will and his nature. Alongside this, the covenant was from the first linked with moral demands in the shape of the Ten Commandments. But the god who makes moral demands of his people must himself be viewed in terms of the demands he makes. Sooner or later the question was bound to press forward: how can suffering be explained in terms of an almighty, all-righteous God?

2

The basic attitude of the Old Testament to suffering is that it is a punishment for sin. In fact the word *avon*, which Cain uses when he says "My *punishment* is greater than I can bear" (*Gen.* 4.13), means both the original sin and the retribution which is inescapably linked with it. So at the beginning of the Old Testament, in *Genesis* (3.14-19), the punishment for Adam and Eve's disobedience is that she shall bring forth children in pain, and he shall have to toil for his daily bread. This is not wholly false; it is a truth, but a partial one. There is a law of life, which we may call if we will the Wrath of God, whereby suffering follows sin, but it does not permit us to draw the line backward from suffering to sin on the part of the sufferer. Hosea puts it well:

> Israel has spurned the good;
> the enemy shall pursue him (8.3).

for there we would see the suffering as the natural consequence of the sin. To Hosea it was still the hand of God: "I will punish them for their ways, and requite them for their deeds" (4, 9). This is the attitude which, as we shall see, Jesus continued to encounter in his own day, and repudiated. It pulsates through the Psalms, perhaps half of which deal with the problem of suffering, though other answers are also adumbrated. It recurs time and again in the prophets.

Of course, it cannot be lightly said. On the one hand the wicked do flourish as the green bay-tree. Here the general picture is one of future retribution:

> But transgressors shall be altogether destroyed;
> the posterity of the wicked shall be cut off.
>
> (Ps. 37.38)

Or as Longfellow, steeped in the Bible as he was, put it:

> Though the mills of God grind slowly, yet they grind exceeding
> small,
> Though with patience he stands waiting, with exactness grinds
> he all.

This thought is very strong in Malachi. Everywhere men are asking, "Where is the God of justice?" and saying, "It is vain to serve God"; but the Lord has his own book of remembrance. Elsewhere it seems even to be suggested that present prosperity is part of God's plan for the wicked, blinding them to their coming destruction:

> How great are thy works, O Lord!
>   Thy thoughts are very deep!
> The dull man cannot know,
>   the stupid man cannot understand this:
> that though the wicked sprout like grass
>   and all evildoers flourish,
> they are doomed to destruction for ever,
>   but thou, O Lord, art on high for ever.
> For, lo, thy enemies shall perish;
>   all evildoers shall be scattered.
>
> (Ps. 92.5–9)

On the other hand the innocent do suffer. Here the commonest explanation lies in our solidarity in sin. We suffer for the sins of our ancestors:

> Do not remember against us the iniquities of our forefathers.
>
> (Ps. 79.8)

So there was current at the time of the Exile a saying that the fathers have eaten sour grapes and the children's teeth are set on edge(Jer. 31.29; Ezek. 18.2), and we did not need Ibsen's Ghosts to tell us that this is true. Jeremiah had a vision (31.30) of a dispensation in which this should be no longer true; that day was not yet. Ezekiel who (surprisingly) shows an even deeper sense of individual responsibility than Jeremiah and roundly asserts: "The soul that sins shall die. The son shall not suffer for the iniquity of the father, nor the father suffer for the iniquity of the son; the righteousness of the righteous shall be upon himself, and the wickedness of the wicked shall be upon himself" (18.20)—even Ezekiel explains suffering corporately. No one more bitterly and passionately denounces the sin of *Jerusalem*, which led to the downfall of *Jerusalem*. "Son of man," God says to him, "make known to Jerusalem her abominations" (16.2), and he does indeed, luridly painting her career of vice and dishonour. There is formal inconsistency here, for by Ezekiel's own stand, God should not punish the present Jerusalem for the misdeeds of former generations: but the inconsistency is only formal, for Ezekiel sees a steady process of sin and suffering marching hand in hand, with God always reaching out in compassion, and as ready in his mercy to restore a repentant Jerusalem as he is bound in his holiness to requite her sins. Ezekiel has two problems to answer. He will not allow his generation to evade responsibility by suggesting that Judah is being punished for the sins of Manasseh, as does the author of *Kings* (2 *Kings* 21.11–15; 23.26–7; 24.3–4; *Jer.* 15.4); he asserts present responsibility. But he must also assert corporate responsibility unless he is to be involved in intolerable paradox. This came naturally to the Hebrew mind, which thought more readily in terms of the calling of Israel, and the incorporation of the individual in the community, than of the calling of the individual, and the establishment of a religious community out of the co-ordination of such individual calls.

The attitude is well exemplified in a Rabbinic story. A number of men were sitting together in a boat, and one of them produced an auger and started drilling into the planks under his feet. The others asked him what he was doing, and he replied abruptly, "That's none of your business; I'm only drilling under myself." But it was their business, for his hole would admit water which would swamp the whole boat.

3

If suffering is consequent upon sin it may be treated as warning rather than as retribution. If I approach my hand to a fire, I feel

pain, and that pain is a warning which may avert the destruction
of the limb. The Old Testament speaks of this as the chastening or
chastisement of God. "It is clear enough", writes one old Testament scholar, "that, in a moral world, evil which defies God and
all His holy purposes must ultimately suffer; it is not less clear that
a Father so wise as God will not spoil the children He loves by
sparing the rod of chastening." Much unfashionable educational
theory incorporates this:

> He who spares the rod hates his son,
>   but he who loves him is diligent to discipline him.
>
> (*Prov.* 13.24)

This is how God treats his children:

> My son, do not despise the Lord's discipline
>   or be weary of his reproof,
> for the Lord reproves him whom he loves,
>   as a father the son in whom he delights.
>
> (3.11–12)

Hosea puts the thought beautifully:

> Come, let us return to the Lord;
>   for he has torn, that he may heal us;
>   he has stricken, and he will bind us up.
>
> (6.1)

So in the *Psalms*:

> Blessed is the man whom thou dost chasten, O Lord.
>
> (94.12)

The thought is taken up in *Job* by Eliphaz:

> Behold, happy is the man whom God reproves;
>   therefore despise not the chastening of the Almighty
>
> (5.17)

and more elaborately worked out by Elihu. It recurs in the New
Testament in *Hebrews*, where the author quotes with approval the
traditional attitude of *Proverbs* (12.5–6), and again in *Revelation*
in the letter to Laodicea: "Those whom I love, I reprove and

chasten; so be zealous and repent" (3.19). There is truth here. Suffering is a discipline which refines and strengthens the soul; manhood is the most precious fruit of trouble. But it is not a sufficient truth, for there is suffering which outstrips the limits of disciplined education. As long as the unit was the nation, the doctrine could stand. Faced with the individualism of Jeremiah and Ezekiel, it was bound to be no more than a partial truth.

4

That suffering is in some sense a punishment for sin is the general view of the Old Testament. To the thoughtful observer, faced with the spectacle of the innocent suffering, this led to one of four conclusions: either he was not innocent, or he was suffering for his father's sins, or he was suffering for the sins of the community, or (though this does not really solve the problem) the suffering is temporary only. To the less thoughtful there were more facile answers. They were, so to speak, backing the wrong horse. "Since we left off burning incense to the queen of heaven and pouring out libations to her, we have lacked everything and have been consumed by the sword and by famine" (*Jer.* 44.18). Even those who held to Yahweh felt that he was behaving like an absentee landlord: "The Lord does not see us, the Lord has forsaken the land" (*Ezek.* 8.12; 9.9). The most remarkable expression of this emotion is undoubtedly the forty-fourth Psalm. The poet knows of Yahweh's past victories, and trusts in Yahweh. Yet Yahweh causes their defeat.

> All this has come upon us,
>> though we have not forgotten thee,
>> or been false to thy covenant.
> Our heart has not turned back,
>> nor have our steps departed from thy way,
> that thou shouldst have broken us in the place of jackals,
>> and covered us with deep darkness.
>
> (44.17–19)

They are not suffering because they have forsaken Yahweh; on the contrary, they are suffering because they have not forsaken

Yahweh. The only explanation can be that Yahweh is asleep and forgetful:

> Rouse thyself! Why sleepest thou, O Lord?
>> Awake! Do not cast us off forever!
> Why dost thou hide thy face?
> Why dost thou forget our affliction and oppression?
> For our soul is bowed down to the dust:
>> our body cleaves to the ground.
> Rise up, come to our help!
>> Deliver us for the sake of thy steadfast love!

(44.23–6)

Here the popular explanation has been transmuted movingly by the gift of song; it remains trivial and shallow.

5

Others who wrestled with the problem at a deeper level were constrained to leave it unsolved. Here the exalted vision of Yahweh's power helped the sense of mystery. "My ways are not your ways, neither are my thoughts your thoughts," saith the Lord. During the period of tension which preceded the fall of Jerusalem there lived the prophet Habakkuk. His opening words lay down the problem:

> O Lord, how long shall I cry for help,
>> and thou wilt not hear?
> Or cry to thee "Violence!"
>> and thou wilt not save?
> Why dost thou make me see wrongs
>> and look upon trouble?
> Destruction and violence are before me;
>> strength and contention arise.
> So the law is slacked
>> and justice never goes forth.
> For the wicked surround the righteous,
>> so justice goes forth perverted.

(1.2–6)

He sees the Chaldaeans amassing, and renews his plea:

Thou who are of purer eyes than to behold evil
    and canst not look on wrong,
Why dost thou look on faithless men,
    and art silent when the wicked swallow up
    the man more righteous than he?

(1.13)

There follows a vivid picture of the imperialist as a fisherman
hauling the nations in his net as a catch, and the great "Woes"
of the next chapter intensify the picture of his economic imperial-
ism, his false security, his brutality and sadism.

To this the answer is that all is in God's hand. The vision is
sure; if it seems slow, wait for it. There is no answer, except that
"My just man shall live by his faith" (2.4), but this is a complete
and sufficient answer for Habakkuk. It is, as we shall see, echoed in
Job, except that to Habakkuk the mystery is bright and the vision
sure, whereas to the author of *Job* the mystery remains dark. It is
the answer Yahweh gives to Jeremiah. The prophet, who does not
doubt that the sin and suffering of Judah go together, still sees the
wicked prospering, and his own words unheeded:

I have become a laughing-stock all the day;
    every one mocks me,
For whenever I speak, I cry out,
    I shout, "Violence and destruction!"
For the word of the Lord has become for me
    a reproach and derision all day long.

(20.7–8)

He is "like a gentle lamb led to the slaughter" (11.19). To him
there is no answer except this:

"If you have raced with men on foot, and they have wearied you,
    how will you compete with horses?
And if in a safe land you fall down,
    how will you do in the jungle of Jordan?"

(12.5)

This was no answer intellectually. God does not justify Jeremiah's
experience of suffering. He simply reasserts that it is part of Jeremiah's mission. Jeremiah had heard God's promise to speak

E

through him and to stand by him (1.7–10). That promise remained. It is in one sense the answer which was given to Habakkuk: "My just man shall live by his faith." In another it was the answer given to Paul: "My grace is sufficient for thee." Jeremiah can indeed still call God *chasidh*, loyal-in-love, as George Adam Smith used to render it. More astonishing, he can comfort Baruch's anguish by a glimpse at the anguish of God in breaking down what he, God, had built up. (45.3–4).

What is notable is its effect on Jeremiah. As Peake has pointed out it did nothing less than transform the conception of religion. "It was this life of unceasing sorrow, this isolation and misunderstanding, that forced the prophet from man to God. To Him he lays bare his troubles, refers his tangled perplexities, utters his keen reproaches or exulting confidence. Beyond other men he is driven into intimate fellowship with God, till it becomes a necessity of his religious life. Thus he came to understand religion as a personal relation between himself and God; thus the individual, not the State, became the religious unit. Here, while his greatest doctrine, that of the New Covenant, still speaks of a covenant made with the nation, yet its fulfilment on Israel's part is guaranteed by the fact that God puts His law in their inward parts, and writes it on their heart, so that for himself each individual knows Him."

6

The most profound passages which concern suffering in the Old Testament occur in the four Servant songs, which appear in the pages of *Isaiah* (42.1–4; 49.1–6; 50.4–9; 52.13—53, 12; there is some minor disagreement as to their exact extent). These are, beyond any doubt, nothing to do with the historical Isaiah; they were, beyond much doubt, composed during the sixth century when the Jews were in exile in Babylon; they were probably the work of the unknown prophet whose sublime monotheism glows from *Isaiah* 40, and whom we sometimes call Deutero-Isaiah. Over their interpretation millions upon millions of words have been spoken, incised, penned, typed and printed; the curious may scrutinize the masterly surveys by Professor North, Professor Rowley and others. The problem arises out of a certain fluidity within the songs themselves. They deal with the Servant of Yahweh: "Behold my servant, whom I uphold" (42.1). In the first song the writer, as often, speaks in the name of God, and writes of the Servant as "he"; in the second he speaks in the name of the Servant, and writes of God as "he". At one moment the Servant is identified with Israel. "You are my servant, Israel, in whom I will be glorified" (49.3); at another the Servant is called by the Lord "to bring Jacob back to him, and that Israel might be gathered to him" (49.5). Furthermore there is the problem of the fourth song, which some have taken as a future prophecy or vision, while others see it as a vividly historical account of one who has died.

The result of this has been that to some interpreters the Servant is a historical individual—Moses, Uzziah, Jehoiachin, Jeremiah, the prophet himself, Cyrus, Zerubbabel, Meshullam or another. To some he is a foretelling of Jesus. There is truth in this, but to think of it as the whole truth is to misunderstand the character of Old Testament prophecy, which is more concerned to forthtell the way of God than to foretell the future. To others he is the personification of Israel, or of a faithful Remnant in Israel. Others yet again see a fluidity of development in the series of songs. If I express a view here it is not with any dogmatism. Clearly the Servant is at one point identified with Israel, but at another conceived as representative of Israel but not identified with her. This is particularly true of the vital fourth song: "He was wounded for our transgressions, he was bruised for our iniquities; upon him was the chastisement that made us whole, and with his stripes we are healed" (53.5). Israel is guilty; she has indeed "received from the Lord's hand double for all her sins" (40.2). The Servant is innocent, and suffers vicariously, redemptively for Israel. Rowley, who sees and senses the individuality of the picture, finds it incredible that it can be other than a future figure depicted. I find it equally incredible that the writer is not writing of an event which has already taken place, and hence of one who has in some sense died for his people. Only one person could in this sense be identified with his people at one moment, and apart from them at another; that is the king. Jehoiachin gave himself up to save Jerusalem from being utterly sacked (2 *Kings* 24.12). We do not know anything about Jehoiachin's death for certain, but we do know that he was released by Evil-Merodach and treated with remarkable honour (2 *Kings* 25.27–30), and it has been plausibly suggested that he was released and fêted in order to be put to death as a royal substitute in the following year. This would accord well with the fourth song. But it remains theory without evidence, and there can be no certainty.

Fortunately, our view of the identity of the Servant does not affect the understanding of the meaning of suffering expressed in these songs, and especially in the fourth of them, and to a lesser extent the third. In these two songs the obedience of the Servant takes the form of a voluntary and humble suffering, not for his own offences, but for the offences of Israel. He offers himself as a kind of guilt-offering, and through his suffering others are redeemed from the power of iniquity.

The first thought about suffering behind these songs is the commonplace that suffering is the natural consequence and punishment of sin. The prophet in whose work these songs are set recurs to this theme again and again (40.2; 42.24–5; 43.22–8; 47.6; 50.1; 51.17–23; 54.6–9). But, this being so, God calls his Servant to transform a situation of alienation, estrangement, iniquity and transgression by freely offering himself to experience the suffering which others have merited and he has not. No explanation is given as to how this willing sacrifice changes the hearts of men. Enough that it does. Enough that this is God's will and God's way. Enough that the vision of God's blessing is as sharply defined as the fact of suffering and death. In short, the second thought is that in a world in which suffering exists as the penalty for doing wrong the innocent are called by God to offer their willingness to suffer in order to bring others back to him. The third great fact shines from the very problem of the Servant's identity: that this is God's way of redemption whether corporately or individually. The Bible knows nothing of one morality for the individual and another for the nation. The doctrine summed up in the catch phrase "Moral Man and Immoral Society" is not merely non-Biblical, it is unbiblical. For the Servant songs deal with the mission of Israel to the nations, and although in the fourth song the Servant, representative of Israel but not identified with Israel, has fulfilled a way which Israel through her disobedience has proved incapable of undertaking, yet there is no difference between God's call to his Servant Israel and God's call to his Servant the representative of Israel. Finally we have an insight which seems quite new. In the fourth song the Servant is to divide the spoil with the strong and to see the fruit of the travail of his soul and be satisfied, because he poured out his soul to death. It is impossible to reconcile an all-loving, all-mighty, all-righteous God with the suffering of the righteous to death, if death is the end. Up to death the fairy-tale ending of *Job* is always, however implausible, a possible answer to the sceptic. At the last, belief in God within a world of suffering means belief in a life beyond the grave, not because, as the Greeks speculated, the soul is by its nature immortal, but because God is just, and loving, and stronger than death. The ultimate answer to suffering lies beyond this world, in the being and nature of God himself.

7

For most people *The Book of Job* offers the last word on the problem of suffering. It is a wonderful dramatic poem, but theologically inadequate, and is nothing at all compared with the vision of the Suffering Servant.

The book as we have it falls into five sections. The first is a rewriting of an old folk-tale. Job is righteous and prosperous. Satan, one of God's servants whose function is to sift and test, argues to God that his righteousness depends upon his prosperity; to remove the prosperity will show that Job is serving God for what he gets out of it. So Satan has permission to test him. First he destroys his prosperity and family; Job's response is "Naked I came from my mother's womb; and naked shall I return; the Lord gave, and the Lord has taken away; blessed be the name of the Lord" (1.20). Satan now lays his hands upon Job's body; his wife tempts him to "curse God and die", but his only response is: "Shall we receive good at the hand of God, and shall we not receive evil?" (2.10). This is the first part. Job has suffered, his suffering does not arise from his sin, but he has so far accepted his suffering unquestioningly.

The second section is an extended dialogue between Job and three friends, Eliphaz, Bildad and Zophar. For a week they sit in silence, then Job breaks out. Perhaps their unspeaking lamentation has got the better of him, perhaps a week's brooding on his innocent suffering has changed him; he now curses the day on which he was born. This leads his friends to speak. Some have tried to differentiate them from one another, and there may be variation of emphasis, but essentially their theme is the same. Job is suffering; therefore Job has sinned. Eliphaz puts it beautifully in his opening speech. Job has always had a word in season for sufferers (evidently calling them to penitence); he must now speak the same word to himself. Who that was innocent ever perished? Can a man be pure before his Maker? No, man is born to trouble as the sparks fly upward. Happy is the man whom God reproves. They press him more and more violently with accusations of secret sin, claiming that God is exacting from him less than his guilt deserves (11.6). Job sings superb songs of despair; his case remains constant. He is blameless (9.20–2). God does not care. Either he is indifferent, destroying innocent and guilty alike (9.22), or he actually favours the wicked (12.6; 21.7 ff.). The government, and therefore the Governor, of the universe is at best amoral and at worst immoral. Even if he, Job, has sinned, his sin is trivial; it does not hurt God. Why should God be such a petty persecutor? (7.17–21). God is his enemy, his adversary; Job takes up Jeremiah's unanswered cry of "Violence!" (19.7; Jer. 20.8), but his conclusion is even bitterer than Jeremiah's, and his justly famed but illogical certainty that his Redeemer or Vindicator lives, and that without his flesh he will see God (the immoral tyrant of the universe?) is no answer to his own complaints. The problem, well posed in the story, has never been so eloquently expounded.

The third section adds nothing to what has gone before, and is patently a later addition. Some later writer felt that the case for orthodoxy had been inadequately presented, and introduced a new figure, Elihu, to restate it. Restate it he does, and no more; he says nothing that the friends have not said before him. For Elihu there is no problem. God is righteous; suffering is the punishment of wickedness; Job has sinned and is adding rebellion to his sin; his chastisement is a warning to him to return from his wickedness. This does not help.

The fourth section is the controversial section. God's presence is revealed in a tremendous storm, and his voice is heard in the tornado: "Who is this that darkens counsels by words without knowledge?" God neither explains nor defends his actions. Instead he knocks Job down with a terrifying display of power and a flood of questions which range in majestic poetry over the whole creation and show Job's utter and humiliating ignorance of the ways of God which he has dared to challenge. Job is brought to the ground; he realizes that he was talking about things too great for him to understand, and repents in dust and ashes. This is the answer of *The Book of Job*: life is a dark mystery, and the ways of God are too exalted for us to understand. The exalting poetry should not blind us to the fact that it is a bad answer. For, in the first place, Job has said "I am insignificant; why should I be punished?" and it is no answer to say "You are insignificant; why shouldn't you be punished?" In the second place, and more seriously, Job has taxed God with immorality, and it is no answer to that agonizing cry, which re-echoes in generation after generation, to say, "I am very powerful; do not question my morals." In the third place, even if it is ultimately true, it is the worst possible pedagogy to answer a child's genuine question with the words, "You are not clever enough to understand." In the fourth place, we are rightly suspicious of a God who speaks out of a whirlwind, and are readier to be persuaded by a still, small voice.

As for the final section, it is utterly lamentable, for now that Job has repented, all his prosperity is restored, and the whole message of the book is vitiated. No problem is left at all.

8

The testing time of the Maccabean Wars called out a theology of martyrdom. In 1 *Macc.* we have the historical account of the sufferings and struggle; in 2 *Macc.* a devotional commentary on the earlier part of the story; in *Daniel* a tract for the times, written to encourage those who were suffering under persecution; and in 4 *Macc.* a philosophical commentary on the events stressing the supremacy of reason over sufferings. Of these *Daniel* is the oldest, being written during the actual events; 1 *Macc.* was probably composed about 100 B.C.; the other two commentaries were rather later, but before the fall of Jerusalem in A.D. 70. 3 *Macc.* is oddly named as it has nothing to do with the Maccabees, but recounts some parallel events in the third century. Despite these variations, it is possible to draw out something like a consistent theology from these books, and Ethelbert Stauffer has done so.

Thus the martyr's death is a sign of his coming victory (*Dan.* 3). The martyr suffers for the name of the one true God and glorifies God in his death (*Dan.* 6.11; 11.32; 1 *Macc.* 1.54; 6.7; 2 *Macc.* 6.1 ff.; 3 *Macc.* 7.16; 4 *Macc.* 8.24). His strength derives from the fearlessness of those that fear God (*Dan.* 3.16–18; 2 *Macc.* 6.26; 7.30; 4 *Macc.* 13.14 ff.). He chooses eternal glory rather than temporal glory (1 *Macc.* 1.66; 3.59; 4 *Macc.* 15). He finds peace through martyrdom (4 *Macc.* 17.19) and is granted a place of honour in the world to come (*Dan.* 12.1–3; 2 *Macc.* 7.9; 7.28 ff.; 4 *Macc.* 5.37; 13.7; 17.18; 18.23).

Underlying all this is something of the thought which the Jews took over from Persia, that life is a conflict between the children of light and the children of darkness. Hence the language used is frequently that of warfare, or of the gladiatorial show, or of boxing and wrestling, or of encounters with wild animals in the arena. The persecutors are described as ravening beasts, and are painted in the language of darkness and tyranny. Meanwhile the whole cosmos watches this spectacle of conflict.

So far there is nothing particularly profound. But we also meet in these books a clear indication that the suffering of the martyrs

might be expiatory. There is no attempt on the part of the martyrs
to take a "holier-than-thou" attitude to their fellows. Thus in the
story of the Seven brothers, the sixth and seventh alike proclaim
that they are suffering for their own sins (2 *Macc.* 7.18; 7.32). But,
that said, they see their death as expiatory for the sin of the whole
Jewish people. Indeed, the words of the youngest brother are
remarkable in that he trusts that his suffering will bring blessings
upon his nation and a change of heart in his persecutor. "But, I as
my brethren, give up both body and soul for the laws of our
fathers, calling upon God that he may speedily become generous
to the nation; and that thou [the persecutor] amidst trials and
plagues mayest confess that he alone is God; and that in me and
my brethren thou mayest stay the wrath of the Almighty, which
hath been justly brought upon our whole race" (2 *Macc.* 7.37 ff.).

So in 4 *Maccabees* (6.28–9; 17.21–7) we can trace these elements:
(*a*) the fact of physical suffering; (*b*) the idea of suffering unjustly
inflicted by persecutors; (*c*) the idea of suffering as justly due for
the sins of Israel; (*d*) the idea that the suffering is borne by those
who are personally innocent; (*e*) the interpretation of suffering as
legal penalty; (*f*) the interpretation of suffering as purificatory and
propitiatory sacrifice; (*g*) the principle of substitution. It is not
altogether surprising that Bertholet (wrongly) thought that the
fifty-third chapter of Isaiah was a song in honour of Eleazar.

9

Judaism never achieved a higher vision of God and his purposes
than through the Prophet of the Exile. In the Talmud, which
represents the developments of thought, mostly in Palestine and
Babylonia, during the period A.D. 100–300, with some extension
before and after, there is little inclination to take up the vision of
the Suffering Servant, no doubt because the Christians had
arrogated it to themselves. Quotations from the fifty-third
chapter of Isaiah are rare, and it is actually omitted from the
prophetical lessons prescribed for Deuteronomy Sabbaths. It is
true that the Christian Justin Martyr (*Dial.* 68, 89) attributes to
the Jews the idea of a suffering Messiah, but this can hardly be

sustained from other sources, and Rabbi Joses the Galilean in the second century A.D. seems unique in his identification of the Messiah with the Suffering Servant. Two passages in the tractate *Sanhedrin* seem to show a suffering Messiah. In one we read that God loaded the Messiah with commands and sorrows like mill-stones (93b); in the other the Messiah sits at the gates of Rome binding and unbinding his wounds (98a). But the interpretation of these passages is uncertain, and whatever their meaning, they stand outside the main stream of tradition.

A strong strand in the fabric of later Judaism has been content to rest in the answer of Habakkuk, Malachi and *Job*, that the Almighty is not to be grasped within the pincers of our petty syllogisms. Suffering is a mystery which we cannot penetrate. The Talmud records Rabbi Jaunai's words: "It is not in our power to explain the prosperity of the wicked or the afflictions of the right-eous." The meaning of this saying has been questioned, but Rabbi Epstein interpreted it to mean: "The exact relation between sin and suffering in this world is not always to be established, but must be left to the righteous and inscrutable will of God."

The belief that suffering is a punishment for sin remains; it is better to be punished before death. But the thought of punish-ment shades over into chastisement and from there into purifica-tion. The strict correspondence between offence and retribution is modified by an overwhelming trust in God's mercy, and by the growth of the idea of disciplinary and educational suffering. "Only for man's good does suffering come upon him, to rid him of what he has done." There is a general belief that suffering borne as chastisement wipes out a man's sin. "Precious are chastisements," said Akiba when visiting Rabbi Eliezer ben Hyrcanus, and went on to show how chastisement brought Manasseh to God (2 *Chr.* 33.10–13). So in the Midrash in *Ps.* 118.18: "Beloved are sufferings, for they appease like offerings; yea, they are more beloved than offerings, for guilt-offerings and sin-offerings atone only for the particular sin for which they are brought in each case, but sufferings atone for all sins, as it says 'The Lord has chastened me sore, but he has not given me over unto death.'" Sufferings, says a commentary on *Deuteronomy*, propitiate God as much as sacrifices—because they hurt more, and so cost more. From this comes the general idea that suffering can ennoble a man's nature and bring him nearer to God; sometimes it appears almost as a passport to heaven. In this way we see two further ideas modifying the correspondence between desert and punishment. These are the growing sense that spiritual communion with God is more to be valued than material prosperity, and the stronger belief in resurrection and the future life.

The high point of this is the *Zidduk haddin*, the confession of the judgment. This consists in the resolve to "love God with all that he has allotted to you, with happiness as well as with suffering", the acknowledgment that suffering is within the providence of God so that suffering becomes man's confession of God. So the acceptance of martyrdom by Rabbi Chanayya ben Teradym, his wife and daughter became a classic *Zidduk haddin*. In the Midrash on *Ps.* 75.1 this is well expressed: " 'We thank thee, O God, we thank thee; thy name is near.' That is, 'we thank thee when thou givest us benefits, we thank thee when thou smitest us: in either case we thank thee, and thy name is near in our mouth.' " That is the confession. It might be expected to lead to a dangerous masochism, but there is no trace of this; rather the note is one of humble resignation combined with a steady awareness of the presence and love of God.

Finally, occasionally a yet deeper note sounds through, that the sufferings of the righteous or innocent are piacular for others. Thus in the tractate *Shabbat* (33b) we read: "In a time when there are righteous men in a generation, the righteous are seized for the generation; if there are no righteous men in the generation, the schoolchildren are seized for the generation." So too Rabbi Joshua ben Levi said: "He who gladly accepts the sufferings of this world brings salvation to the world."

The teaching of the Talmud on suffering has been summarized under five propositions:

Him whom the Lord loves he chastens hard in order to purify him.
The glory of God draws near to him who is afflicted.
God raises him whom he afflicts.

Sufferings atone more than sacrifice.
Sufferings are a path of life.

Simon ben Yochai said: "The best which God gave Israel, he gave through suffering."

10

Suffering has been written deep into the life of the Jewish nation across the centuries; there is no more moving expression of this than André Schwarz-Barth's magnificent novel *The Last of the Just*.

> "And praised. Auschwitz. So be it. Maidanek. The Eternal. Treblinka. And praised. Buchenwald. So be it. Mauthausen. The Eternal. Belzec. And praised. Sobibor. So be it. Chelnino. The Eternal. Ponary. And praised. Theresienstadt. So be it. Warsaw. The Eternal. Wilno. And praised. Skarzysko. So be it. Bergen-Belsen. The Eternal. Janow. And praised. Dora. So be it. Neuengamme. The Eternal. Pustkow. And praised. . . ."

Well did Sholem Asch cry: "God be thanked that the nations have not given my people the opportunity to commit against others the crimes which have been committed against it." Well did George Eliot in *Daniel Deronda* quote Leopold Zunz:

> If there are ranks in suffering, Israel takes precedence of all the nations—if the duration of the sorrows and the patience with which they are borne ennoble, the Jews are among the aristocracy of every land—if a literature is called rich in the possession of a few classic tragedies, what shall we say to a National Tragedy lasting for fifteen hundred years, in which the poets and the actors were also the heroes?

Well did the eighteenth-century Pulnoer Rebbe compare his people with particles of sand, each separate and distinct, and requiring the fire of calamity to fuse them into one. Well did Jedaiah ben Abraham, four hundred years before, compare time with a frail narrow bridge without handrails, spanning a tempestuous sea. Well did Yehudah Halevi, nearly two centuries before that, seeing his people

Thrust into Christendom, cast out into Islam,
Tested in the furnace of Greece, afflicted under the yoke of Turkey,

see suffering as the hallmark of all individuals and groups called to exceptional service, the lack of power as compensated by the achievement of martyrdom, and the Jewish people's suffering as an essential part of Jewish and human destiny. Well did the greatest of modern Jewish poets, Chaim Nachman Bialik, equip his poems with such titles as *The Dead in the Desert* or *In the City of the Slaughtered*. For Bialik suffering is a challenge to hatred not to love; his message at the last is destructive not constructive. But in his younger days he had a notable vision of life through suffering depending upon the patient waiting for God, as in *The Fountain*.

And shouldst thou wish to know the Source
From which thy tortured brethren drew
In evil days their strength of soul
To meet their doom, stretch out their necks
To each uplifted knife and axe,
In flames, on stakes to die with joy,
And with a whisper, "God is One",
To close their lips?

And shouldst thou wish to find the Spring
From which thy banished brethren drew,
'Midst fear of death and fear of life,
Their comfort, courage, patience, trust,
An iron will to bear their yoke,
To live bespattered and despised,
And suffer without end?

And shouldst thou wish to see the lap
Whereon thy people's galling tears
In ceaseless torrents fell and fell,
And hear the cries that moved the hills,
And thrilled Satan with awe and grief,
But not the stony heart of man,
Than Satan's and than rock's more hard?

And shouldst thou wish to see the Fort
Wherein thy fathers refuge sought,

And all their sacred treasures hid,
The Refuge that has still preserved
Thy nation's soul intact and pure,
And when despised, and scorned, and scoffed,
Their faith they did not shame?

And shouldst thou wish to see and know
Their Mother, faithful, loving, kind,
Who gathered all the burning tears
Of her bespattered hapless sons,
And when to her warm bosom they came,
She tenderly wiped off their tears,
And sheltered them and shielded them,
And lulled them on her lap to sleep?

If thou, my brother, knowest not
This mother, spring, and lap, and fort,
Then enter thou the House of God,
The House of Study, old and grey,
Throughout the sultry summer days,
Throughout the gloomy winter nights.

At morning, midday, or at eve;
Perchance there is a remnant yet,
Perchance their eye may still behold
In some dark corner, hid from view,
A cast-off shadow of the past,
The profile of some pallid face,
Upon an ancient folio bent,

Who seeks to drown unspoken woes
In the Talmudic boundless waves;
And then thy heart shall guess the truth
That thou hast touched the sacred ground
Of thy great nation's House of Life,
And that thine eyes do gaze upon
The treasure of thy nation's soul.

And know that this is but a spark
That by a miracle escaped
Of that bright light, that sacred flame,
Thy forbears kindled long ago
On altars high and pure.

Well may this prayer be prayed: "God of freedom, Thy children still groan under the burden of cruel taskmasters. Slavery debases their bodies and minds, and robs them of the enjoyment of Thy bounties. The fear of cruelty and the peril of death blight the souls of men. O break Thou the irons that bind them. Teach men to understand that by forging chains for others they forge chains for themselves, that as long as some are in fetters no one is truly free. Help them to see that liberty is the very breath of life and that only in the atmosphere of freedom can truth, prosperity, and peace flourish. Imbue us with courage to guard our heritage of freedom above all material goods and to preserve it for others so that all men shall dwell together in safety and none shall make them afraid. Fervently we pray for the universal springtide in the life of mankind when the long winter of intolerance and hatred shall have passed, the vision of the prophets been fulfilled and the glory of Thy kingdom acknowledged of all men. Amen."

There is a wonderful, and true, story told by Tillich in one of his sermons; it emerged during the Nuremberg War-crime Trials. At Wilna in Poland a number of Jews who had escaped from the gas-chambers hid in a graveyard and lived there. There, surrounded by the dead, a young woman gave birth to a boy. The midwife was the gravedigger, an old man of eighty. When the baby let out its first cry the old man offered a prayer: "Great God, hast Thou finally sent the Messiah to us? For who else than the Messiah Himself can be born in a grave?" Three days later the child was sucking his mother's tears because she had no milk for him.

5

The Witness of the
New Testament

1

The New Testament is in one way or another the story of Jesus Christ and his works, and the central fact in the Christian tradition is that Jesus was crucified. So that we are brought sheer against the fact of suffering. It was a shocking fact. Paul gave a reminder to the Corinthians that the Cross of Christ was a stumbling-block to the Jews and folly to the Greeks, and before long the Docetists were claiming that Jesus never suffered at all and that it was all an illusion. They were a minority. Orthodoxy believed that Jesus suffered, that his suffering was in itself a triumph, and that he gave meaning to all suffering, and showed the way to pass through it to victory.

We begin from the Gospels. Not because they are the oldest Christian documents—they are not—but because they present to us Jesus most directly. It is elementary to say that they are not biographies, and the form-critics have done much to enlighten us about the way in which the traditions took shape and were moulded by the needs and practice of the early Church, till we have almost tended to forget that were they not rooted and grounded in fact there would have been no Church at all, early or late. We see Jesus through them, Jesus as he was presented through the life and worship of the Church, and through authors who have their own predilections and concerns. But behind the change worked by time and human fallibility stands Jesus himself. This fact is more important than the divergences between the gospel writers, important though those are. It is indeed an interesting and worthwhile study to single out the characteristic emphasis of each gospel-writer. Thus Mark's gospel has been called the "martyr-gospel", and it has been argued that his object was to strengthen the Christians of his day to face persecution in the knowledge that Jesus suffered, that he warned them that those who followed him would suffer, and that the steadfast acceptance of suffering would lead to fullness of reward. Again Luke has his own concern with suffering, being a doctor. But it seems better here to put together the thoughts which are common to all the gospels.

The first clear fact that shines through the gospels is that suffering is to be healed. Jesus's first discourse in his own synagogue at Nazareth was upon the text "The Spirit of the Lord is upon me, because he has anointed me to preach good news to the poor. He has sent me to proclaim release to the captives and recovering of sight to the blind, to set at liberty those who are oppressed, to proclaim the acceptable year of the Lord" (*Luke* 4.16 ff.). We need not list all the works of healing which Jesus performed. But we may note that when John sent from prison to ask Jesus "Are you he who is to come, or shall we look for another?" Jesus's answer is "Go and tell John what you hear and see: the blind receive their sight and the lame walk, lepers are cleansed and the deaf hear, and the dead are raised up, and the poor have good news preached to them" (*Mark* 11.2 ff.). In one healing story suffering is seen as the work of Satan, which Jesus undoes (*Luke* 13.16). All this is to be seen in the context of his proclamation that the Kingdom of God, that is the reign or sovereignty of God, is at hand (*Mark* 1.15). As the kingdom of God, the age of the Messiah, comes with power, disease, suffering and death itself are conquered. These are part of the limitations of the unfulfilled world. It is right and natural that the first fruits of Pentecost should have been a deepening sense of community and a new power to heal (*Acts* 2.43–3.10). It is right that the vision of the last things, which ends the New Testament, should contain the words: "Behold, the dwelling of God is with men. He will dwell with them, and they shall be his people, and God himself will be with them; he will wipe away every tear from their eyes, and death shall be no more, neither shall there be mourning nor crying nor pain any more, for the former things have passed away" (*Rev.* 21.3–4). Suffering has its place in the purposes of God, otherwise it would not exist; but it has no place in God's ultimate purposes.

Secondly, Jesus gives no assent to the idea that suffering is a punishment for sin, which was a commonplace theory of the time. It is true that the healing of the sick of the palsy (*Mark* 2.1–12; *Luke* 5.17–26; *Mark* 9.1–8) might seem to give countenance to the view that disease is the requital of sin. Jesus first pronounces the man's sins forgiven (because of his friends' faith), and then demonstrates the forgiveness by showing that the man is physically healed. But it is a very different matter to diagnose a particular illness as psychosomatic, and to assert that disease is a punishment for sin. In any case the point of the story (though not the point of Jesus's healing act) is the demonstration to the watching scribes and Pharisees *on their own terms* that the Son of Man has power to forgive sins. By their own beliefs the healed body demonstrated the healed spirit. Elsewhere, however, Jesus makes explicit his denial that disease and death are the punishment for sin. "Do you think that these Galileans were worse sinners than all the other Galileans, because they suffered thus? I tell you, No" (*Luke* 13.2–3). Montefiore's remark, that he "does, if only incidentally, set some limit to an exaggerated application of the doctrine of the divine retribution" is a grotesque understatement; an American scholar has put it more justly when he says: "While the New Testament constantly argues from sin to consequent trouble, it never argues from trouble back to sin as a necessary formula of explanation." Even more explicit is the passage in St. John's Gospel about the healing of the man blind from birth (*John* 9.1 ff.). The disciples, imbued with current beliefs, asked whether his blindness was due to his own sin or that of his parents. Jesus's answer is flat: "It was not that this man sinned, or his parents, but that the works of God might be made manifest in him." The negative side of this elenchus is important. The New Testament is not interested in abstract questions about the origin of suffering, but in the way in which suffering can be made the opportunity of glorifying God.

Thirdly, Jesus saw his own destiny as taking him to suffering

and death. This was part of God's plan, as Peter declared at Pentecost (*Acts* 2.23). But in order to understand what this meant we
must see it in context. To the Jew life was one and life was whole.
Israel, says Manson, "is a complex organic whole which includes
the monotheistic faith, the cultus in Temple and Synagogue, the
law and custom embodied in the Torah, the political institutions
which had grown up in the post exilic period, the claim to owner-
ship of the Holy Land, and whatever dreams there may have been
of an Israelite world rule to supersede the rule of the Gentile
empires." For the Jew this cause of Israel was a single and indivi-
sible thing. This is the context of the Messianic hope, the context
in which Luke, the most politically eirenic of early Christian
writers, recorded the utterance of those revolutionary songs
Magnificat and *Benedictus*. The Messiah was looked for as the
successful leader of the revolution and thereafter a ruler of irresis-
tible wisdom, power and justice. As Manson says, the very idea of
a crucified Messiah was a stumbling-block to the Jews; but the
idea of a successful Messiah in this other sense was equally a
stumbling-block to Jesus. Three times Jesus received the title of
Messiah, and three times Jesus rejected the way of violent victory
and worldly success for the way of suffering. The first was at the
Temptation (*Mark* 4.1–12; *Luke* 4.1–13). "If you are the Son of
God . . ." says the Tempter, and the climax of the Temptation in
Matthew's narrative is to achieve the Messianic kingdom by the
Tempter's method, which were the methods of the Zealots and
the war of liberation. This, and the other temptations, he rejects
—and comes down with the proclamation that the kingdom of
heaven is at hand. That kingdom is in man's obedience, not in
man's power. The second key-moment was Peter's confession at
Caesarea Philippi (*Mark* 8.27–33; *Matt.* 16.13–23; cf. *Luke*
9.18–27). Peter declares him the Messiah, and he does not reject
the title, but goes on to say that the Son of Man must suffer and be
killed. "And he said this plainly." Peter protests at this, and by his
words "Get behind me, Satan", Jesus makes it clear that he sees
this as a recurrence of the Temptation. The third and final test is
at the trial and execution, where the High Priest (*Mark* 14.61),
Pilate (*Mark* 15.2) and the mockers at the Cross (*Mark* 15.32) all

offer him the Messianic title, and he bears it to the Cross.

There was of course scriptural precedent for the hope of a conquering Messiah. "Ask of me," says the Psalmist (and the reference to this in the Temptation is inescapable), "and I will make the nations your heritage, and the ends of the earth your possession. You shall break them with a rod of iron, and dash them in pieces like a potter's vessel" (*Ps.* 2.8–9), and Zechariah has an oracle to much the same effect (*Zech.* 12.7–9), while in the non-canonical scriptures, and above all in the 17th Psalm of Solomon, the idea is rampant. So strong was the conception that the title of Messiah was sufficient to form a capital charge with the Romans, and it may well be that Dibelius is right in seeing the anointing of Jesus by the woman with the alabaster vase (*Mark* 14.3–9) as an anointing of the Messianic King, and the grounds of Jesus's arrest. Jesus, we have seen, rejected this view of the Messianic King. Instead, he picked up other passages of scripture. There was, for example, another oracle of Zechariah (*Zech.* 9.9–10), prophesying (as George Caird puts it) "that one day a king would come to Zion, riding on a donkey to show that his authority rested not on military force, but on his ability to establish a reign of universal peace". But above all Jesus identified— for the first time as far as we can see—the Messiah with the Suffering Servant of God who appears in the later chapters of Isaiah. For the first time. This has been questioned, but the confusion of the disciples is sufficient proof. "It is no exaggeration to say," wrote Wheeler Robinson, "that this is the most original and daring of all the characteristic features of the teaching of Jesus, and it led to the most important element in His work. There has been no success in all the endeavours made to find previous or contemporary identification of the Messiah with the suffering servant of Yahweh." "Jesus," said J. W. Bowman, "and he alone, was responsible for the fusion of the two prophetic concepts." Here Manson's words are so eloquent and just, that they merit full quotation: "Jesus had discovered and made his own the foundation principle of all thinking about the kingdom of God and of all working for it; a proposition childishly simple and constantly overlooked by the strong and wise, who have it in mind to bring in a kingdom *for* God. *In the kingdom of God God is King*. He had accepted fully all the consequences that follow when this proposition is taken seriously: for example, that the messianic task is to be the servant of the Lord *par excellence*; that the servant of the Lord must work in God's way of merciful redemptive love; that he must be the 'friend of publicans and sinners'; that he must proclaim a kingdom of God that is a ministry of this kind, and cannot be anything else." His Ministry is throughout, in Von Hügel's word, a costing ministry. Of this Ministry the sacrifice and the suffering are the logical conclusion, the Servant's supreme obedience, the perfect manifestation of the mercy and love of God, the only way in which that mercy can at the last meet its enemies—and meet them victoriously—seeing that God is Love. "The sacrifice and suffering of the Son of Man are not the prelude to triumph: properly understood they are the supreme triumph."

Fourthly, this way has been laid not only upon Jesus, but upon all who follow him. This is in fact implicit in his repeated words that "the Son of Man must suffer". Manson has shown that "Son of Man" is a symbolic title which Jesus took from the book of Daniel, where it stands for "the people of the saints of the Most High" (*Dan.* 7.13–18). It is in fact a composite title. This is itself important, for it has sometimes been suggested that this way of obedience through suffering is valid in individual but not in corporate relationships. Nothing is further from the mind of Jesus. It is true that at the last the rest fail, and he stands out as the one faithful representative of the people of the saints of the Most High, and the true Son of Man. But that is not implicit in his thought, and the disciples do in fact later learn to enter into the fellowship of his sufferings.

> And all through life I see a cross—
>   Where sons of God yield up their breath;
> There is no gain except by loss,
>   There is no life except by death.

Jesus repeatedly gives warning that discipleship involves suffering. When a scribe offers to follow him, he answers, "Foxes have holes, and birds of the air have nests; but the Son of Man has nowhere to lay his head" (*Matt.* 8.19–20; *Luke* 9.57–8). He promises them the cross; if they do not take it, they are incapable of learning from him (*Matt.* 10.38; *Luke* 14.27; cf. *Mark* 8.34; *Matt.* 16.24; *Luke* 9.23). James and John come to him and ask for places of honour in the Kingdom. His answer is that they must drink the cup of suffering and be baptized with the baptism of death; and he goes on to point the fact that to be a disciple means to be a servant (*Mark* 10.35–45). In *John* the theme of the Servant is dramatically depicted when Jesus washes the disciples' feet. He goes on to tell them to wash one another's feet. He knows that they will not stand the test now, but he knows also that they will come to be strong, and promises them hatred and persecution and death. "Remember that word that I said to you, 'A servant is not greater than his master.' If they persecuted me, they will persecute you" (*John* 15.20). All this is closely linked with the positive way of love, and the presence of the Spirit of God—the Advocate— with them. But the key to it is seen in the Beatitudes. "Blessed are those who are persecuted for righteousness's sake, for theirs is the kingdom of heaven" (*Matt.* 5.10). To be persecuted *for the sake of righteousness* is to be in the kingdom, for the simple and sufficient reason that it is to be obedient to God as King. "This is the way the Rule of God works: there is no alternative way," wrote Manson, and added, "And it does work. The Crucified Messiah is the great undefeated figure in world history." His followers share his victory.

Finally, there are the great apocalyptic predictions of suffering (*Mark* 13; *Matt.* 24; *Luke* 21). The same thought may be present earlier when, after John was put in prison, Jesus came, not with words of gloom and disaster, but preaching the good news of the kingdom of God (*Mark* 1.14). Here we have a new idea, that suffering is part of travail, and that these are the birthpangs of a new age (*Mark* 13.8; *Matt.* 24.8). This thought is not original with Jesus. Similar phrases are found in the prophets (e.g. *Isa.* 26.17; 66.8–9; *Jer.* 22.23; *Hos.* 13.13; *Mic.* 4.9–10), sometimes in the immediate context of the expectancy of the Messianic Age, and the idea later became a commonplace of the rabbis, probably it was already in the nature of a technical term. Still, it is important that Jesus, who was selective in what he adapted from tradition, chose to adopt this.

We are now in a position to attempt some sort of summary.

Jesus did not seek to explain the fact of suffering, and rejected facile explanations given by others. In God's mysterious providence suffering is a fact of life in a world which is incomplete because it is not given over in full obedience to God as king. The love of God reaches out to heal such suffering. But suffering being a fact, it can still be turned to the glory of God. God's way is not to meet violence and sin with violence and sin but with suffering and love. God brings in his kingdom not as the conquering commander but as the suffering servant. God turns alienation to atonement by suffering. Suffering, which is a fact of life, can be inflicted wantonly and cruelly, as Pilate inflicted it on the Galileans; it is then, in the strict sense, meaningless. It may be a fact of nature while this world has not reached its fruition; the task of the Christian disciple is to allay and heal it. But it can also be used redemptively. Sin seeks to conquer love by inflicting suffering; love conquers sin by accepting that suffering. This is a hard saying to worldly wisdom, but to the Christian the cross is the symbol of its truth.

2

It is temerarious to seek to say something in a small compass about Paul's thought on any matter, let alone something as central as suffering: but the attempt must be made. In so doing, we are assuming the authenticity of the letters usually attributed to him.

The first fact to realize is that Paul was no armchair philosopher speaking about suffering from the secure seclusion of a study. He spoke of what he knew. As he tells the Corinthians in a famous passage (2 *Cor.* 11.23–9): "Are they servants of Christ? I am a better one—I am talking like a madman—with far greater labours, far more imprisonments, with countless beatings and often near death. Five times I have received at the hands of the Jews the forty lashes less one. Three times I have been beaten with rods; once I was stoned. Three times I have been shipwrecked, a night and a day I have been adrift at sea; on frequent journeys, in danger from rivers, danger from robbers, danger from my own people, danger from Gentiles, danger in the city, danger in the wilderness, danger at sea, danger from false brethren; in toil and hardship, through many a sleepless night, in hunger and thirst, often without food, in cold and exposure. And apart from other things, there is the daily pressure upon me of my anxiety for all the churches. Who is weak, and I am not weak? Who is made to fall, and I am not indignant?" Reading the passage again, one recalls Adlai Stevenson's remarks about later disciples of Christ: "Anyone who travels in Africa is constantly reminded of missionaries' heroism. They laid a groundwork in religion, health and education under difficult and dangerous circumstances. What they have done is almost beyond belief. They fought yellow fever, dysentery, parasites—and the gravestones I saw! My God, their gravestones—all through Africa!" Paul, like those who followed his path centuries later, knew what it was to suffer.

Secondly, Paul sees the whole of creation as subjected to frustration. Up to and including the present, he says, the whole of creation has been joining in sounds of pain, and mankind shares in that pain. The passage, one of the most glorious Paul ever wrote (*Rom.* 8.18 ff.), is also one of the most difficult and controverted; even the punctuation is uncertain. But one thing is clear. Paul does not explain evil by means of an anti-God. However hard it is to accept, the limitations, frustrations, incompleteness and travail of the world we know are there by the will of God. To that word "travail" we shall return. For the moment let us note that Paul does not deny suffering—how could he?—that he sees it as a sign of the incompleteness of the present stage of the world, and that he accepts that limitation as part of the will of God which he does not attempt to explain. "It is a superb passage," writes Professor Raven; "one of those outreaches of sheer inspiration in which from time to time the Apostle is lifted. . . . Here is no doctrine of a Devil able to pervert God's good purpose, nor of any total depravity of nature and man. Here is no excuse for the dark subtleties of the doctrine of election and those grim verdicts upon the reprobate with which 'Paulinism' has so largely been concerned. Here is such a picture of the love and sufficiency of God as is the authentic flowering of the 'root of Jesse', the firm foundation for a Christian and incarnational philosophy."

For, thirdly, this is no play enacted with God as a remote spectator—in what we still call "the gods". God redeems us by sharing in our suffering. He is an actor, not a looker-on. His Spirit comes in alongside us and shares in our agony with groaning too deep for words. This is the thought which Paul applies to Jesus in that other magnificent passage which opens the first letter to Corinth. God is the source of our life, in Jesus Christ, who by being crucified became in the eyes of the world foolish and weak, but who, to those who will enter the new life he offers, is wisdom and strength. "God was in Christ, reconciling the world to himself" (2 Cor. 5.19). God redeems us by coming alongside us and sharing in the suffering which is part of our inescapable lot in this world. So in a third passage of surpassing splendour, in *Philippians 2*, Paul gives a picture of Jesus drawn from the Suffering Servant of *Isaiah* 53; the key words are "Servant", "humbled himself", "emptied himself", "exalted". But Paul deepens the picture. For he sees Jesus as having the power to cling on to Godhead, but refusing, and emptying himself for the sake of men. This is the great cry of "Immanuel", "God with us". This is why the passage in *Romans* ends in its breathless climax: "Who shall separate us from the love of Christ? Shall tribulation, or distress, or persecution, or famine, or nakedness, or peril, or sword? As it is written

> For thy sake we are being killed all the day long;
> we are regarded as sheep to be slaughtered.

No, in all these things we are more than conquerors through him who loved us. For I am sure that neither death, nor life, nor angels, nor principalities, nor things present, nor things to come, nor powers, nor height, nor depth, nor anything else in all creation, will be able to separate us from the love of God in Christ Jesus our Lord" (*Rom*. 8.35–9).

But we are not done yet. We suffer, being involved in an imperfect and incomplete world. God comes in alongside us and shares our suffering, redemptively. He now calls on us to share his suffering. Paul here shows how he has understood the Master whom he only came to know too late to hear his teaching, but who told his disciples, "If any man would come after me, let him deny himself, and take up his cross and follow me" (*Mark* 8.34). So Paul seeks to share in the fellowship of Christ's sufferings (*Phil.* 3.10). He suffers with Christ (*Rom.* 8.17), is crucified with Christ (*Gal.* 2.20), dies with him (*Rom.* 6.8), is buried with him (*Rom.* 6.4), and is raised and lives with him (*Rom.* 6.8). To die with Christ and so to live with him is the common lot of the Christian (2 *Tim.* 2.11). It is true that there is in some of this an allusion to the sacrament of baptism (*Col.* 2.12; 2.20). But there is something deeper and more far-reaching than that. In writing to Colossae, Paul makes a vast claim: "Now I rejoice in my sufferings for your sake, and in my flesh I complete what is lacking in Christ's afflictions for the sake of his body, that is the Church" (*Col.* 1.24). There is a sense in which Christ's work is complete. God's self-giving on the Cross has taken place. The victory is won. The kingdom of this world has become the Kingdom of our God and of his Christ. Yet we have only to look at the world to see that Christ's work is incomplete. The creation is still in pain, still waiting for the revelation of God's children. And just as we still crucify Christ by our sin, just as the Lamb, slain from the foundation of the world, is slain till its dissolution, so the work of redemption through suffering goes on, and we are called to share in it. It must be so; for to Paul the Christian's life is the life in Christ; Paul uses this phrase or its equivalent 164 times. Once or twice he dares to put it the other way round: "And this secret is simply this: Christ *in you*! Yes, Christ *in you* bringing with Him the hope of all the glorious things to come" (*Col.* 1.27, Phillips; cf. *Gal.* 2.20). "The religion of Paul," says Deissman, "is something quite simple. It is communion with Christ." "This personal union with Christ," says Garvie, "is the constant dominating factor in the religious experience and moral character of Paul." Not only of Paul, "Union with Christ," writes Mackintosh, "is a brief name for all that the apostles mean by salvation. For St. Paul and St. John oneness with Christ is to be redeemed, and to be redeemed is oneness with Christ." So Paul uses the glorious word *koinonia*, or fellowship. "God is faithful by whom you were called unto the fellowship of his Son, Jesus Christ our Lord" (1 *Cor.* 1.9). This fellowship, as we have seen, is the "fellowship of his sufferings" (*Phil.* 3.10). So he tells the Corinthians that God has reconciled us to himself through Christ and entrusted us with the ministry of reconciliation (2 *Cor.* 5.18–19). The ministry is the same ministry, and to fulfil it we must expect to suffer.

It follows that the Christian will rejoice in his Christlike sufferings, not only for what they promise, but for what they are. Paul rejoices in his sufferings *for the sake of others*, because he is completing what is lacking in Christ's afflictions, that is because he is continuing the work of Christ for others (*Col.* 1.24). The same thought shines through the "letter of joy", the letter to Philippi. Through his sufferings, he rejoices in the Lord and calls on them to rejoice. The same thought underlies a familiar passage in *Romans*. There he specifically says that "we rejoice in the hope of sharing the glory of God. More than that, we rejoice in our sufferings, knowing that suffering produces endurance, and endurance produces character, and character produces hope, and hope does not disappoint us, because God's love has been poured into our hearts through the Holy Spirit he has given us" (*Rom.* 5.2–5). "We also rejoice in God through our Lord Jesus Christ, through whom we have now received our reconciliation" (*Rom.* 5.11). Here his joy starts from the promise, the hope of something new, but soon is carried over into the joy in the knowledge of the presence of God's Spirit alongside him in his suffering, his certainty that he is sharing in the at-onement with Jesus.

But there is a future promise also in Paul's thought about suffering, and to see it at its highest we must turn back to the great passage in *Romans* 8. There the pain of the created universe was seen as a sign of its incompleteness. But it is also a sign of its coming to fruition, its pregnancy, its childbirth. "The process," writes Raven, the most profound expositor of this passage, "is one of eager expectation. Nature, like a young wife waiting for her firstborn, makes ready for the coming of the child that is to be. When the days are complete, God's family will be born upon the earth. In their manifestation the agony of the ages will find its fulfilment and its justification."

3

For our present purposes it does not matter deeply whether the so-called first letter of Peter is rightly attributed or not. What matters is that it is shot through and through with the Christian understanding of suffering.

Peter starts from Jesus Christ. He uses a number of different images of Christ and his saving work. He clearly identifies him with the Suffering Servant of *Isaiah* 53. "He committed no sin; no guile was found on his lips. When he was reviled, he did not revile in return; when he suffered, he did not threaten; but he trusted to him who judges justly. He himself bore our sins in his body on the tree, that we might die to sin and live to righteousness. By his wounds you have been healed. For you were like straying sheep, but have now returned to the Shepherd and Guardian for your souls" (2.22–5). In the middle of that comes the phrase, "He bore our sins in his body on the tree" (2.24). This is not from *Isaiah*, but from *Leviticus*. In the Atonement ritual the High Priest took a goat, laid his hands upon the animal's head, and in this attitude confessed the sins of the people transferring them to the scapegoat, which then bore all their iniquities away to the wilderness (*Lev.* 16.6–10; 16.20–2). At another point Peter explicitly identifies Jesus with the Passover lamb (1.19). As the blood of the Passover Lamb kept the Israelites safe from the angel of death in Egypt, so the blood of Jesus Christ keeps those whom Peter is addressing safe from the consequences of their futile acts. Through all these images runs the theme of vicarious suffering. In God's eternal providence the suffering of Christ transforms the situation on earth, and creates a new situation of hope, faith, confidence, freedom, security.

This is why Peter continually links the suffering of Christ with his glory (1.11; 1.21; 4.13; 5.1). This is why he starts from the resurrection (1.3). For to Peter the presence of God's power in Christ, the suffering, the resurrection and the glory are not separate, but united. The glory is yet to be revealed, but it is there all along. Suffering undertaken in the power of God is the gateway to new life. "If you are reproached for the name of Christ, you are blessed, because the spirit of glory and of God rests upon you" (4.14). Where God's power is, the glory is in the suffering and the suffering leads to the glory. So too in Luke's Gospel the suffering and the glory are linked (*Luke* 24.26).

The Christian disciple follows his Master. "For to this you have been called, because Christ also suffered for you, leaving you an example, that you should follow in his steps" (2.21). To share in suffering under God is not just to copy Christ, but to share in his work (3.17–18), and because it is to share in his work it is to share in his glory, and therefore a cause for rejoicing (4.13–14; 5.10).

Peter then submits the suffering of the Christian to a rigorous analysis.

First, the Christian must expect to suffer. The letter begins and ends on that note (1.6; 5.9). Plainly it was written at a time of persecution. But the words are not mere consolation; they are part of the expectation that those who are one with Christ will pass along the way of Christ, and the Master's words were cited in the early Church in that expectation (*Matt.* 10.24–5).

Secondly, not all suffering is redemptive. Suffering is viewed by Peter as part of our inescapable environment in a world which has gone away from God. Suffering is to Peter sometimes the proper consequence of doing wrong (2.14; 2.20; 3.17; 4.15). There is no credit in such suffering. The suffering to which Christ calls us is suffering for doing right (2.20; 3.17), suffering as being a Christian (4.16). The Christian must do what is right, freely, as God's servant (2.15–16), no matter what the consequences; in that suffering the glory of God is seen (4.16). "Therefore let those who suffer according to God's will do right and entrust their souls to a faithful creator" (4.19).

Thirdly, such suffering is a test, a fiery ordeal (4.12). A faith which has stood the test of suffering is like gold which has been refined in the fire (1.6–7). Peter does not say that God sends suffering in order to test us, but that suffering is among the circumstances of life, and does in fact provide a testing-ground. So too

James says, "Count it all joy, my brethren, when you meet various trials, for you know that the testing of your faith produces steadfastness" (*Jas.* 1.2–3).

Fourthly, the fullest and profoundest of the several accounts of the place of suffering in the Christian life comes in a context which demands careful examination. It is part of an injunction to slaves not to react violently against their overlords, however tyrannical; and this follows closely on an injunction to all subjects to submit freely to Rome's imperial rule. (The connection, we may note in passing, would have special relevance in the reign of Domitian at the end of the first century, for he claimed to be *dominus* to his subjects, which was equivalent to saying that all inhabitants of the Empire were in effect the Emperor's slaves.) That is to say that the philosophy of suffering, if we may so call it, is a social philosophy not just an individual stance.

Fifthly, one remarkable verse sees suffering as the common experience which binds together the Christian brotherhood. "Resist him [that is, the devil] firm in your faith, knowing that the same experience of suffering is required of your brotherhood throughout the world" (5.9). Perhaps we should not read too much into this. Perhaps it is only expressing the fact of widespread persecution. (If so, unless it expresses an expectation which was not immediately fulfilled, it can hardly belong to the age of Nero.) On the face of it the words imply a little more than that, not an accident of history so much as a vocation of suffering.

Sixthly, suffering is, as we have already seen, the gateway to glory, for as the power of God in Christ, Christ's suffering, his resurrection and his glory are ultimately all one and the same, so for the Christian who follows and is one with his Master, God's power, suffering for Christ and the right, rebirth to new life, and glory are all linked together (4.14). No cross, no crown is only the negative of *Ubi crux, ibi lux* (*Mark* 8.34–5; *Matt.* 16.24–7; *Luke* 9.23–4). This is why the Christian, confronted with suffering, rejoices (1.6) and is enjoined to rejoice more (4.13), because by this road the full glory of Christ is revealed to him. This association of joy and suffering is typical of the early Church. James, as we have just seen, calls his readers to count it joy to meet trials (*Jas.* 1.2).

The author of *Hebrews* tells how Jesus "for the joy that was set before him endured the cross" (*Heb.* 12.2). Luke tells how the apostles rejoiced that they were counted worthy to suffer dishonour for the name (*Acts* 5.41). Jesus himself, after all, had said: "Blessed are you when men revile you and persecute you and utter all kinds of evil falsely against you on my account. Rejoice and be glad, for your reward is great in heaven" (*Matt.* 5.11–12).

We spoke just now, tentatively, of the philosophy of suffering. It is important to see that Peter, near as he comes to it, does not quite work it out. He is clear that Christ's suffering is, in the mysterious purposes of God, redemptive, that God used the obedient suffering of Christ, in a way which Peter can explain only by analogy, to break the chains which hold men to a life of sin and futility with all its consequences. He is clear that the Christian must do that which is right, in faith. He goes beyond this, and identifies the Christian life with the life of love (1.22; 3.8), which does not return evil for evil (3.9), but meets wrong with right, abuse with blessing, and unjust power with suffering. He is clear that the Christian who lives in this spirit will receive suffering, partly because he is alienated from those who hold the power in the world, partly because the whole brotherhood of Christians, being one with Christ, must expect to suffer with Christ. He is clear that such suffering is by the will of God, and the glory of God that gleams through it will shine more brightly for them beyond the grave. One thing and one only is lacking—the sense that the suffering undergone by the Christian is part of the purposes of God in changing *this* world.

4

The thought behind the letter to Hebrews comes out of the whirlpool of Alexandrian Judaism, and the suggestion that it came from Prisca and Aquila is as likely as any, though in no sense certain. We are even less certain who were the recipients. All we know is that they had faced and endured persecution in the past, but were wavering in the present. To restore their faith the writer presents to them Jesus—Jesus the Son (1.2, etc.), Jesus "on whom faith depends from start to finish" (12.2 *N.E.B.*)

In the presentation of Jesus the writer puts forward a very remarkable doctrine of suffering, which is worked out carefully and fully. He speaks of Jesus as the Son, and quotes passages of scripture which he takes to refer to Jesus. He sees in *Psalm* 8 a foretelling of what Paul terms the self-emptying of Jesus (*Phil.* 2.7), and goes on to describe him as "crowned now with glory and honour because he suffered death, so that by God's gracious will, in tasting death he should stand for us all. It was clearly fitting that God for whom and through whom all things exist should, in bringing many sons to glory, make the leader who delivers them perfect through sufferings" (2.9–10 *N.E.B.*).

"Perfect through sufferings." These words, as Theodore Robinson has rightly said, contain the centre of the writer's thought. He does not mean that Jesus was, apart from his death, morally imperfect. The word "perfect" means "complete", "grown-up". But what does this mean? It is as the "author of our salvation" (*A.V.*) that Jesus is made complete through sufferings. In other words, he could not help us to salvation, pioneer the road for us, did he not first suffer. Why not? Plainly, in part, because if he did not suffer he would not stand where we stand. The road would be useless because we would never reach it. It would be like the motorway soaring across the countryside with no means of access. Suffering is a condition of our humanity. Why, is a great mystery. We may not, with some Eastern religions, dismiss suffering as an illusion. We may not, either, regard all suffering as chastisement; we have already seen the Hebrew mind in revolt against this. Perhaps it is a condition of our freedom; to be really free implies a world in which things can go wrong. Whatever the cause, it is a fact of human experience, and if Jesus did not share in that fact, he would be aloof from us.

But there is a second thought in this passage, which we may see if we take up a second passage couched in closely similar language. "Because of his humble submission his prayer was heard; son though he was, he learned obedience in the school of suffering, and, once perfected, became the source of eternal salvation for all who obey him" (5.7–9 N.E.B.). Here there is the thought that suffering is needful to our well-being as humans. We all know the people who would be frankly better for a bit of suffering. It would extend their sympathies. But, more than this, suffering is a school. It is a discipline, which passes through pain to joy (12.7–11). The author is here picking up thoughts which we have already met among the Greeks, of the close association between suffering and learning (*pathos* and *mathos*), and of the need for training (*ascesis*). It is this which on the human level constitutes the writer's chief encouragement to his readers. He tells them that sons are always disciplined by their fathers, and if they received no discipline of suffering they would not be true sons of God. He is not saying in this that without suffering there would be no disapprobation of wrongdoing, that suffering is the thorny hedge which keeps us from straying off the road. This thought is, as we have seen, found in the Bible. But the thought here is almost the diametrical opposite. The road itself passes through thorns, and we must be trained to stick to the road. What we learn is obedience; what we reach is joy.

Where the author of *Hebrews* is so daring is in applying this thought to Jesus himself. He dares to say not merely that Jesus had to be made perfect through sufferings (2.10), but that he learned obedience (5.8), and that he "for the sake of the joy that lay ahead of him, endured the cross, making light of its disgrace" (12.2). This is the converse of what we have seen before. Jesus suffered to make the bridge between him and us. But if his fullness was only to be found in suffering, he is our exemplar in all things. If to be a true son of God means to suffer, then the unique Son must suffer supremely. In *Hebrews* this suffering is seen at its deepest, not at Calvary but in Gethsemane. Here "in the days of his earthly life he offered up prayer and petitions, with loud cries and tears, to God who was able to deliver him from the grave" (5.7). Here he learned obedience, and because of his humble submission his prayer was heard.

Go to dark Gethsemane,
Ye that feel the Tempter's power;

Your Redeemer's conflict see,
Watch with Him one bitter hour:
Turn not from His griefs away,
Learn of Jesus Christ to pray.

We may agree with Montgomery in following out the thought of
Hebrews to the cross; for there too Jesus passed through "My
God, my God, why hast thou forsaken me" to "Father, into Thy
hands I commend my spirit", and because of his humble submission his prayer was heard.

The long central section of the letter takes up some of these
ideas in technical language which means less to us than to the
original recipients. In this section Christ appears as the high priest.
But "the blood of his sacrifice is his own blood, not the blood of
goats and calves; and thus he entered the sanctuary once and for
all and secured an eternal deliverance. For if the blood of goats
and bulls and the sprinkled ashes of a heifer have power to hallow
those who have been defiled and restore their external purity, how
much greater is the power of the blood of Christ; he offered himself without blemish to God, a spiritual and eternal sacrifice; and
his blood will cleanse our conscience from the deadness of our
former ways and fit us for the service of the living God" (9.12–14
N.E.B.). The thought is alien to us, but there is no need here to
examine it in detail; its outline is clear. What is important for our
purpose is this. Christ offers his own blood, that is his life, to
convict our consciences and draw us back to God. That life is in
the first place without blemish, because, as we have learnt, he was
made perfect through sufferings. In the second place the very
offering can be made only through suffering. Life can be offered
only through death. At two different levels Christ's self-offering
involves suffering.

This leads to our final point, and in it we may be going beyond
the conscious insight of the writer of *Hebrews*, though not beyond
what is implicit in his words. To the Christian Jesus shows us both
God and man. God shares our suffering. If this were not so, the
bridge would be broken and our faith would be vain. But is this
not a necessary corollary of our affirmation that man is made in

the image of God? If this be true, are we not bound, in some sense, to see God's image in man? The old taunt recoils on the taunters. We cannot believe in an impassible God. Theodore Robinson has put it superbly. "May we not venture further still? It is not given to man to assert with confidence what is, and what is not, necessary to the experience of God. Yet we may reverently conjecture that personality, whether human or divine, will have certain features and characteristics wherever it appears. And we know from our own experience that suffering means an enlargement of personality. One who has suffered greatly is not necessarily better than he would otherwise have been, but his nature is certainly more complete. We cannot avoid the feeling that one who has never suffered would be incompletely human. May it not, then, be equally possible that the experience of suffering is essential to the divine nature, that even God would not be God unless He knew pain? If so it would follow that the higher any individual stands in the order of being, the more necessary it is that he should suffer, and that Jesus, who stands so far above all else, should be made perfect only through suffering." We have said that this view is implicit rather than explicit, but at one point it comes near to a direct statement. The writer assails those who, although they have once seen the light, fall away. These, he says in pungent phrase, "crucify Christ anew". So Donne picks up his words:

> Spit in my face you Jewes, and pierce my side,
> Buffet, and scoffe, scourge, and crucifie mee,
> For I have sinn'd and sinn'd, and onely hee,
> Who could do no iniquitie, hath dyed:
> But by my death can not be satisfied
> My sinnes, which passe the Jewes impiety:
> They kill'd once an inglorious man, but I
> Crucifie him daily, being now glorified.

Does not this mean that God for ever suffers? That there is a cross at his heart? Was not the creation itself a crucifixion? Is not the Lamb slain from the foundation of the world?

6
The Witness of the Church

1

"The blood of Christians," wrote Tertullian in celebrated words, "is seed" (*Apol.* 50). This was factually and unpredictably true. We can trace in the unsympathetic narrative of Tacitus (*Ann.* 15, 44) something of this; he says that Nero's brutality towards the Christians led the bystanders to pity them, despite their guilt. Tertullian himself, if we may judge from incidental passages in his writings, was converted by the example of the Scillitan martyrs in A.D. 180. These courageous men and women were ready and unflinching when the call came. One of the women gave her simple testimony in the witness-box, "I am a Christian" (*Christiana sum*) and on hearing the sentence of death, "Thanks be to God" (*Deo gratias*). Their bearing in face of death moved Tertullian. "No one would have been willing to be killed unless he was in possession of the truth," he wrote (*Scorp.* 8). Pliny had spoken of the obstinacy of the Christians. In his defence of the faith Tertullian wrote: "That very obstinacy with which you taunt us, is your teacher. For who is not stirred up by the contemplation of it to find out what there is in the thing within? Who, when he has found out, does not draw near? And then, when he has drawn near, desire to suffer, that he may receive all forgiveness from him in exchange for his blood" (*Apol.* 50). Again he wrote many years later to Scapula: "None the less this school will never fail—no! you must learn that then it is built up the more when it seems to be cut down. Every man who witnesses this great endurance is struck with some misgiving and is set on fire to look into it, to find what is its cause; and when he has learnt the truth, he instantly follows it himself as well" (*ad Scap.* 5).

Equally significant was the martyrdom of Polycarp, bishop of Smyrna, in 155. The proconsul demanded that he recant and revile Christ. The old man replied: "I have served him for eighty-six years, and he has done me no wrong; how can I blaspheme my Saviour and Emperor?" (*Mart. Pol.* 9). They tied him to the stake, and he offered his last prayer: "Lord God Almighty, Father of Thy beloved and blessed child Jesus Christ, through whom we have received full knowledge of Thee, God of angels and powers and of all creation and of the whole family of the righteous who live in Thy presence! I bless Thee, that Thou hast counted me worthy of this day and hour, that among the roll of the martyrs I may share in the cup of Thy Christ, for the resurrection to eternal life of soul and body in the incorruption of the Holy Spirit. May I today be received in Thy presence among them, a rich and acceptable sacrifice, as Thou, the God in Whom is no falsehood and all truth, hast prepared beforehand, revealed beforehand and fulfilled. Therefore for all things also I praise Thee, I bless Thee, I glorify Thee through the eternal heavenly high priest Jesus Christ, Thy beloved child, through whom be glory to Thee with him and the Spirit both now and for all time to come. Amen" (14). The narrator has earlier spoken in general terms of the bearing of the martyrs (2), their nobility, endurance and love of their Master. He tells how their endurance of cruelty moved some of the by-standers to pity, and how by their patience under suffering they won eternal life. He now applies his general conclusion to Poly-carp (19). "Such was the story of the blessed Polycarp, who, though with those from Philadelphia he was the twelfth martyr in Smyrna, is unique in being especially remembered by all, so that he is spoke of in every place, even by the heathen. He was not only a famous teacher, but also a notable martyr, whose martyr-dom all desire to imitate, for it followed the gospel of Christ. By his endurance he overcame the unrighteous ruler, and thus gained the crown of immortality, glorifying God the Almighty Father, rejoicing with the apostles and all the righteous, and he is blessing our Lord Jesus Christ, the Saviour of our souls and Governor of our bodies, and the Shepherd of the Universal Church throughout the world."

In all these accounts of martyrdom we can trace a common pattern of interpretation. In the first place, Jesus is the prototype of Christian obedience. We have seen this in the New Testament. "If a man would come after me, let him deny himself and take up his cross," said Jesus (*Mark* 8.34), and the cup of suffering and baptism of death were the necessary conditions of the disciple's sharing his Master's glory (*Mark* 10.37 ff.). "The man who confesses Christ," writes Stauffer, "is taken up into the fellowship of Christ's sufferings; indeed his destiny is conformed to the death of Christ. Hence the desire to emulate Christ must prove itself in a readiness for an *imitation* of his passion." So Ignatius writes to the Ephesians (10.3): "Let us be eager to be imitators of the Lord and seek who may suffer the more wrong, be the more destitute, the more despised," and to the Romans (6.3): "Permit me to be an imitator of the passion of my God." So too Polycarp's martyrdom is drawn out in careful parallelism with the passion of Jesus. He waits to be betrayed as the Lord had done. He stays outside the city with a few friends in prayer. He is betrayed by those whom he trusted. The chief of police is called Herod. They go out as against a robber. He faces the Roman governor, respects his authority but points out that it comes from God. After his execution he has a dagger thrust into his side. So, as we have seen, his martyrdom is said to follow the gospel of Christ. Eusebius also likes to develop the parallel between the passion of the martyrs and the passion of their Master (*HE* 2, 23, 20 ff.; 5, 1–2).

Secondly, martyrdom is seen as a skirmish or episode in the battle between the powers of light and the powers of darkness. This is not explained, but two features of it are clear. On the one hand the obedience of the martyrs to God, their refusal to compromise, their faithfulness even to death are the necessary condition of their share in God's victory. On the other hand to take life is the typical weapon of the powers of darkness, to suffer death is the typical weapon of the powers of light. So the suffering of the martyr is portrayed in terms of a contest. We see this in Clement of Rome (1 *Cl.* 5, 1 ff.; 7, 1), Ignatius (*Pol.* 1, 3), *The Martyrdom of*

Polycarp (18, 3), Tertullian (*Mart.* 3) and even much later in Augustine (*C.D.* 14, 9). This is in fact the underlying pattern of Eusebius's account of the first three centuries of Christendom. They are the centuries of conflict; his history is a history of the Church under the cross (*H.E.* 5 *prol.*). In this battle the confessors defeat the persecutors, the victims overpower the executioners, the dead are stronger than the living. There is a power here which the calculations of worldly wisdom has never understood; it is beyond calculation, for it is God's power, and it is victorious against all the odds.

Thirdly, the martyr's crown is for him the crown of glory. It is the gateway to eternal life. This is clear in *The Martyrdom of Polycarp* (2) where the author says that the martyrs knew Christ at their side sustaining them during their ordeal, that through his grace by a single hour they purchased eternal life and passed into the company of the angels. *The Shepherd* of Hermas (*Vis.* 2, 2, 7, *Sim.* 9, 25, 2) also suggests that those who walk in righteousness and in particular those who endure persecution become one with the angels. So Ignatius in writing to the Romans again and again expresses his conviction that through his martyrdom he will attain to God (1, 2; 2, 2; 4, 1). "Let me make a meal for the animals," he writes: "through them I can reach God. I am God's wheat, and I am ground by the teeth of animals so that I may be found Christ's pure bread." So too martyrdom is depicted frequently in Tertullian's words (*Bapt.* 16) as "a second baptism, a baptism of blood", which washes the sin of the martyr. Eusebius calls it a "baptism of fire" (*H.E.* 6, 4, 3). This element is particularly strong in the account of the martyrdom of Perpetua and Felicitas (21). Martyrdom is an expiation (*Acts of P. and Th.* 34; Mel. Sard. *fr.* 12). It is important to realize that it is not the blood of the martyrs which avails for expiation, but the blood of Christ in whose sufferings the martyrs are caught up.

But there is another element in these accounts of martyrdom. This is the redemptive element. Paul has proclaimed himself to the Corinthians a kind of expiatory sacrifice (1 *Cor.* 4.13). This language is taken up by other early writers, by Barnabas (6.5) and Ignatius (*Eph.* 8, 1; 18, 1). The letter of Ignatius to the Ephesians is here especially notable. Not merely does he offer himself as an expiatory offering for the church at Ephesus, which was not his home-church. But his words go beyond this, and he thinks also of the persecutors (10): "Pray unceasingly for other men—for there is in them a hope of repentance—that they may find God. Permit them to become your disciples, at least through your actions. Be gentle in face of their fury, be humble-minded in face of their proud words, offer prayer in face of their blasphemy, be firm in faith in face of their wanderings from the truth, be gentle in face of their cruelty, and do not seek to retaliate. By our gentleness let us be proved their brothers. Let us be eager to be imitators of the Lord, and seek who may suffer the more wrong, be the more destitute, the more despised." So, just as Stephen, following his Master, cried at his death, "Lord, do not hold this sin against them", so the blood of the martyrs is a cry of intercession for the sins of others (Eus. *H.E.* 2, 23).

2

One particular story of martyrdom speaks with especial clarity of the way in which God uses the obedience of suffering to change history. The gladiatorial displays were a running sore on the face of Rome. They titillated the sadism of the spectators who must have spent a large portion of the year in a state of aberrant sexual excitement. Humanists might protest, but they did little about it. During the period of the Roman Republic the gladiatorial fights had not spilled over on to public festivals, but they were a frequent feature of funeral celebrations and of election campaigns, and the story of Spartacus reminds us that the gladiators *en masse* were a formidable army. Cicero speaks of the fights as "that kind of spectacle to which all sorts of people crowd in the greatest numbers, and in which the multitude takes the greatest delight" (*Sest.* 59, 125). Even the humane Cicero did not disapprove in principle, though he thought that in practice they were becoming too cruel. With the Empire the shows grew to an appalling extent. The growth of public holidays for the celebration of spectacles of various kinds is one indication; in the reign of

Augustus there were 66 a year, under Marcus Aurelius 135, and in the fourth century 175 or more. The Flavian amphitheatre, which we call the Colosseum, would seat some 45,000 spectators; it was inaugurated with exhibitions lasting for 100 days. Trajan's triumph in Rumania was celebrated by 123 days of festival, during which 10,000 gladiators appeared in the arena (D.C. 68, 15). Nor was it only at Rome. At Pompeii there was a barracks for gladiators. In the small town of Fidenae the amphitheatre collapsed and 50,000 spectators were involved in the disaster (Tac. Ann. 4, 62). From many minor Italian towns we have records of munificent gladiatorial shows sponsored by wealthy citizens. They spread from Italy as the Romans spread. Alexandria had its school of gladiators, Tunisia and Gaul their mighty amphitheatres; even in the wilds of Pisidia there were gladiatorial fights at Antioch. Few voices were raised in protest. In Athens, faced with the proposal to introduce the shows, the philosopher Demonax said, "First overthrow the altar of Pity", and Dio, Plutarch and Lucian made their witness against the brutality. At Rome, Seneca made his protest: "Man, an object of reverence to men, is now slaughtered for jest and sport" (Ep. 95, 33 cf. De Brev. Vit. 13). Seneca was one of the few who acted. He lacked the power—or the courage—to abolish the shows, but in the early days of Nero's reign, when he was regent, the lives of the vanquished were for once spared. Another who acted was a magistrate of Vienne, named Trebonius Rufinus, in Trajan's reign. He abolished the shows in Vienne, and protests reached the emperor; the name of Junius Mauricus should be remembered for supporting the abolition (Plin. Ep. 4, 22). Such men were a pitiful minority. In general the lust of the crowd had its way, and the aristocrats were no better. Tacitus, in attacking the blood-lust of Drusus, himself speaks contemptuously of the "cheap" life of the gladiator (Ann. 1, 76). Centuries later one of the last great exponents of philosophic paganism, the cultured Symmachus, went to great expense to secure a company of Saxon gladiators to celebrate his son's appointment as praetor. They preferred suicide to exposure as a public exhibition, and Symmachus has no word of pity or understanding, only a bitter contempt (Ep. 2, 46). The very coming to power of Christianity made little difference. Constantine expressed a certain distaste in a proclamation to the East (*C. Th.* 15, 12, 1); in the West there was little or no check. Theodosius might ban worship in the pagan temples; he did not ban the blood-sport of the arena. Prudentius, here more Christian than most, pleaded with the emperor Honorius to put an end to the slaughter of men as his father had put an end to the sacrifice of bulls (*C. Symm.* 2, 1124). But words counted for nothing.

The "games" were being celebrated in the Flavian amphi-theatre. The people were there in their tens of thousands. The nobles were there. The emperor was there. And there was a monk named Telemachus. We know little about him but his name. He acted where others had talked. In protest against man's inhumanity to man, he interposed his body between the swords of the gladia-tors. They cut him down on the spot, amid the jeers and plaudits of the crowd whose cruel sport he had dared to interrupt. But God moves in a mysterious way His wonders to perform. The passion of Telemachus moved Honorius where the pleas of Prudentius had failed, moved the weak Honorius to act where strong men like Constantine and Theodosius had failed to act. That was the last occasion in which the gladiatorial display was held in Rome.

> His dream became a deed that woke the world,
> For while the frantic rabble in half-amaze
> Stared at him dead, thro' all the nobler hearts
> In that vast Oval ran a shudder of shame.
> The Baths, the Forum gabbled of his death,
> And preachers linger'd o'er his dying words,
> Which would not die, but echo'd on to reach
> Honorius, till he heard them, and decreed
> That Rome no more should wallow in this old lust
> Of Paganism, and make her festal hour
> Dark with the blood of man who murder'd man.
>   (Tennyson: *St. Telemachus*)

3

Pietro Bernardone's son Giovanni was born at Assisi in the early 1180s while his father was on a business trip to France, as a result of which he gave his son the additional name of Francesco, by which posterity has known him. Francis grew up as a young-man-about-town, and something of a trial to his father. Life as a prisoner-of-war broke his idle ways. Released, he returned to them. Illness brought the first crisis of conversion. The second came from a pilgrimage to Rome. The religious life of the capital touched him not at all, except to realize that the pilgrims who claimed so much were giving so little. What moved him was the spectacle of hordes of beggars. He began to ask whether the call of God was not merely to succour suffering humanity but to take their burden upon himself and be identified with them.

From this point he turned from his earthly father to his heavenly Father. He stripped himself of all possessions, and went out to labour in his Father's vineyard. He sustained himself by manual labour or through alms; his real work was to preach the gospel of repentance. Repentance, yes; but Francis's gospel was a gospel of joy and love and peace in the midst of a world where lust for power reigned, and men were as wolves to one another. How could this be?

First because his life was God-centred, and he saw God in Jesus Christ sharing the sufferings of men. It is well known that Francis set up the first Christmas crib at Creccio. We tend to equate this with Albert bringing to Britain the first Christmas tree. The Christmas crib has become a sentimental prettiness for the children's corner of the church. It was not so to Francis. Here was a solemn and yet joyous message—to children, for he loved children, and to ordinary worshippers, but also to episcopal potentates and learned theologians: "Behold your God, a poor and helpless child, with ox and ass at his side."

This gave him his vision of perfect joy. Not holiness, not the gift of healing, not prophecy, not the understanding of God's world, not even the power to preach so as to change men's lives.

This is perfect joy—to share the sufferings of the world, as Christ did. "When we arrive at Santa Maria degli Angeli, soaked with rain, frozen with cold, covered with mud, dying of hunger, and we knock and the porter comes in a rage, saying, 'Who are you?' and we answer, 'We are two of your brethren,' and he says, 'You lie, you are two lewd fellows who go up and down corrupting the world and stealing the alms of the poor. Go away from here!' and he does not open to us, but leaves us outside shivering in the snow and rain, frozen, starved, till night; then, if thus maltreated and turned away, we patiently endure all without murmuring against him, if we think with humility and charity that this porter really knows us truly and that God makes him speak thus to us, then, Brother Leo, write that in this is the perfect joy."

From this came Francis's deep sense of brotherhood which led him, in response to his Master's example, to identify himself with others. The rich merchant's son had wedded his Lady Poverty; and his proudest title was *poverello*, the little poor man. He identified himself with the leper by kissing his wounds. The wolf was his brother; death was his sister. *The Canticle of the Sun* is his hymn of praise in words, but first he lived it.

But how to transform a world of war, and power, and cruelty, and hatred, and worldly wisdom, and "political realism"? There was the message—the message to those in power that the Son of Man came not to be ministered to, but to minister; the message to war-crazy petty principalities and embattled Christendom that the climactic title of the child in the manger was "Prince of Peace" and that this Prince of Peace blessed the peacemakers, condemned the works of the sword and entrusted to his followers the ministry of reconciliation; the message to those who hated their fellows that in being born a man Christ made all men his brothers, and brothers of one another, the message that God had created all creatures and all men to be brothers, and that if he could have a wolf for his friend, surely human beings could love one another. But the message alone was not enough. In Francis's renunciation of the world there was something of the old Cynic attitude. Possessions do disturb the peace of mind; Jesus said it as well as Diogenes. When the Bishop of Assisi said that he thought that to lack possessions must be a harsh and difficult way of life, Francis rejoined, "My lord, if we possessed property we should have need of arms for its defence, for it is the source of quarrels and lawsuits, and the love of God and of one's neighbour usually finds many obstacles therein; this is why we do not desire temporal goods." The man who was unburdened by possessions was set free to love and to joy in the life of love. But the whole burden must go, and Francis would not claim for himself, did not allow the brethren to claim, and in his testament continued to forbid, any protection of any kind from the Roman *curia*. In this way freedom from possessions was exposure to the worst the world could do. Francis knew this; in one sense he renounced the world, in another he embraced it. He laid no claims upon it, but he allowed it to claim him. He knew that to transform, to redeem the world required a heart ready to accept the world in its entirety, and to offer itself as an unsullied sacrifice. It was to take up the Cross.

The *stigmata* are in fact central to our understanding of Francis. We are learning more about the power of mind over matter, and there is nothing for the rationalist to doubt, while to the faithful they remain a miracle, because the gift of God. During the 1939–45 War a man was brutally bound and maltreated by the Gestapo and left for dead. He was nursed back to some measure of physical health but remained a neurotic wreck. In seeking to help him they hypnotized him and asked him to project himself back to the prison-camp. Immediately, the deep weals of the ropes appeared on his wrists and ankles. Francis spent a lifetime in contemplation of Christ crucified. His service of man was his Master's. His way of transforming the world by sacrificial love was his Master's. He was in Christ. He was making up that which was lacking to the sufferings of Christ. Towards the end of his life marks corresponding to the five wounds of Christ appeared on his body. There was no exhibitionism in Francis. He kept the manifestation dark from even his most intimate disciples. But they meant much to him, and he died with left hand upon the wound in his side, saying, "I have done what I had to do; may Christ teach you what is your part."

4

Of all the leaders of that complex movement we call the Reformation, none understood the ministry of suffering better than
Conrad Grebel. Grebel belonged to Zwingli's Zurich. Zwingli is
of course much better known than Grebel in the pages of history,
but although he had outstanding gifts of intellect and leadership,
he compromised with political power and appears a lesser man.
Yet he at one time had a clear vision of the suffering Church.
Oswald Myconius, a friend of Zwingli, was persecuted in
Lucerne for his faith. Zwingli wrote to him: "There will always
be people who will persecute us Christians because Christ is in
us. . . . I believe that just as the church was born in blood, so it can
be renewed only by blood, not otherwise. . . . Never will the
world accept Christ, and even the promise of rewards by Christ
is accompanied by the promise of persecution. He sent out His
own like sheep among wolves." Zwingli lost his vision and forgot
his faith, or this aspect of it, but he and Myconius had a common
friend in Grebel, who did not forget. Grebel and his friend Felix
Manz were university students at Zurich, and members of a
Bible-study group with which Zwingli was also associated. They
had a great admiration for Zwingli's personality, but when
Zwingli, nominally continuing to uphold the authority of
Scripture, in practice subordinated Church to State, their ways
parted. Grebel challenged Zwingli publicly, and their views
proved utterly irreconcilable. Grebel's studies in the Bible now
led him to a further step. He could not find any Scriptural justification for infant baptism, and with his associates ceased to
practise it, when Zwingli and the City Council had ruled that it
should be retained. The intensity of Zwingli's hostility to Grebel
suggests that he saw in Grebel his own better conscience. In the
winter of 1524-5, Grebel and his friends were ordered to quit
Zurich; they held a defiant service of believers' baptism, but
obeyed the order. By November 1525, however, Grebel and
Manz had returned, and were imprisoned for their disobedience.
In March 1526 the City Fathers placed a rigid ban on services of

rebaptism, with the bitterly appropriate punishment of death by drowning. Grebel in fact died of plague, but Manz was judicially drowned, the first of the Anabaptist martyrs, and another of the group was burnt at the stake. H. A. Bender, our chief authority on Grebel, remarks coolly but justly: "The further history of the Anabaptist movement became chiefly a record of martyrdom."

In the story of Conrad Grebel and his associates we see men who clung to their convictions come wind come weather. Rufus M. Jones in his *Studies in Mystical Religion* wrote judiciously of the vision of the Reformers: "Those who had this vision, and with it had the power of restraint, and the gifts of statesmanship to see what would *work* and what would not work in the world as it actually was then, became the leaders of the Protestant Reformation and have their renown in the pages of history. Those who had this vision and who were resolved to *make the world fit for the vision*, with no shade of levelling down and with no hairs-breadth of compromise, became the leaders of Anabaptism, risked everything for the cause they believed in, flung out ideals which have been guiding stars for us ever since, went to death in terrible fashions, and fell on almost total obscurity." Dr. Geoffrey Nuttall, from whose knowledgeable, incisive and challenging writings this account of Grebel is derived, has said that an unsympathetic observer might be tempted to say that the acceptance of suffering by the Swiss Brethren was no more than stark realism; there was nothing else that they could do; even so, it represented an advance on resentment and the spirit of retaliation. But, as Dr. Nuttall equally makes clear, this is the very least that can be said of Grebel and his friends. When Thomas Münzer was repudiated by Luther, as Grebel had been by Zwingli, Grebel, Manz, Andres Castelburger (the leader of those who rejected war as sin and incompatible with the Gospel) and others wrote him a letter in these terms: "The Gospel and those who accept it are not to be protected by the sword, nor are they to protect themselves. . . . Truly believing Christians are sheep among wolves, sheep for the slaughter; anguish and affliction, tribulation, persecution, suffering and death must be their baptism; they must be tried with fire, and must reach the fatherland of eternal rest, not by killing their bodily, but by mortifying their spiritual enemies." Grebel added a postscript commentary on Münzer's encouragement of the Peasants' Revolt: "If thou art willing to defend war, then I admonish thee . . . that thou cease therefrom. . . . And if thou must suffer for it, know well that it cannot be otherwise. Christ must yet more suffer in His members. But He will strengthen and keep them steadfast to the end."

This was the core of Grebel's thought. Professor Bender has well said: "It is noteworthy that Grebel bases his rejection of the sword and war and of killing as a whole, not upon the specific teaching of the Sermon on the Mount"—which he never quotes once in his extant writings—"but upon the thought of the suffering church." There is here no philosophy of suffering; there is rather a deep sense of obedience to the call of God as expressed through Scripture, and the clear certainty that this means the rejection of violence and the acceptance of suffering. God calls the Church to suffer, as he called Christ to suffer. We do not know why; it is ours to obey the call, and leave the rest to Him. This is faith.

5

Two stories of martyrdom from recent times will show that still today the blood of Christians is seed. Both come from Africa and date from the last century. Christian missionaries reached Madagascar in 1818. By 1831 it was estimated that there were some two thousand converts, and that perhaps 30,000 of the islanders had come within range of Christian influence. But in 1835 there came to the throne Queen Ranavalone I, and there followed more than a quarter of a century of bitter and largely unremitting persecution. In 1839 the order was given that all Christians should be seized, bound, thrown in a pit, should have boiling water poured over them and should be buried on the spot. Again in 1849 there were eighteen death sentences, and over 2,000 Christians were sentenced to other penalties such as flogging and enslavement. Yet the Christians stood firm. The cruel queen herself was moved to astonished and reluctant admiration. "I have killed some," she said, "I have made some slaves till death, I have put some in long and heavy fetters, and still you continue praying. How is it that you cannot give that up?" Her very officers used to say to one another, "Let us go and see how these Christians behave; they are not afraid to die." A spectator who watched some Christians at the stake in 1849 left his record: "They prayed as long as they had life. Then they died, but softly, gently. Indeed, gentle was the going forth of their life, and astonished were all the people around that beheld the burning of them."

In 1861 the queen died, and her successor Radama II proclaimed religious liberty. From bush and forest and wilderness and cave and mountain the Christians reappeared as if risen from the dead, and as they came back they sang the old pilgrim-song, "When the Lord turned again the captivity of Zion we were like them that dream." Then the incredible truth emerged. The Christians were many times more in number than they had been before the persecution started. The witness of the martyrs had borne fruit; their blood had proved to be seed. Radama's successor Radavalona II was baptized in 1868, and in the following year destroyed the palace-idols, and commended Christianity to her people. There were already 50,000 members, and three times that number of adherents. Now there were 1,500,000 more hungry for the Word of Life.

At Bonny in what is now Nigeria, among the creeks of the Niger delta, the persecution did not last so long, but it was very bitter and in one respect was even more dramatic. It was in Bonny that the first African bishop of modern times, Samuel Ajayi Crowther, and his son Dandeson had extirpated the sacred lizards and their worship. The pagan priests were for the moment helpless, but growled and bided their time, working up underground opposition to the Christians, especially in private consultation with the chiefs. Eventually they saw their chance and pounced. The occasion was the baptism of new converts. Among the new converts was a slave-boy who took the Christian name of Joshua. His owner was one of the chiefs, who went by the name of Captain Hart. They took Joshua to make him renounce his new-found faith. The test of the renunciation would be a willingness to eat food offered to idols. Captain Hart first commanded, then threatened. Next came direr action. First the boy was beaten. Then, when that had no effect, a gang of men took hold of him and flung him high in the air, letting his body fall, bruised and broken, on to the ground. Still the boy declared that he would work as hard for his earthly master as his powers allowed, but he would not eat flesh offered to idols. It was Polycarp over again, but this boy had not lived in his heavenly master's love for eighty-six years; he had only just been baptized. But he knew what commitment meant and he stood firm by his commitment. Now they bound him hand and foot and took him out in a canoe, and flung him into the waters of the Niger. They pulled him out half-drowned and told him that this was his last chance to renounce his faith and live. Joshua, like Stephen before him, prayed Jesus's own prayer, prayed it to Jesus himself: "Forgive them, for they do not know what they are doing." "You be praying again," cried Captain Hart, and picked him up helpless as he was and threw him into the water again. This time as Joshua's body came to the surface they beat him over the head with a paddle and pierced him with a sharp pole through and through.

Joshua was the first martyr of many. Some were staked out in the open and bitten to death by ants. Some were starved rather than eat meat offered to idols. Some died in chains. For three years persecution continued. Then came the strange feature of the story. A man rose up in the council of chiefs and pleaded for tolerance and the end of persecution. That man was Captain Hart. He pleaded well, and the persecution was ended. The Christians came back from their hiding-places in creek and bush, as they did in Madagascar, and, as in Madagascar, it was seen that they were more numerous than before. The revived church grew and flourished, and a few months later the former slave-owner and murderer, Captain Hart, followed into baptism the man whom he had murdered.

6

It would be possible to adduce many people in whom a capacity for sainthood has arisen out of a capacity for suffering. It may be useful to select one who is less known in this country. This is Brother André of Montreal. His name was Alfred Bessette, and he was born in 1845, one of a family of twelve. He grew up the hard way. The family was poor, and they were often hungry; their food was of the simplest. When Alfred was only nine his father, a wheelwright, died through an accident in the timberyard; two years later his mother, a loving and devoted woman, followed. Young Alfred went from one job to another—shoemaker, baker, farmhand, blacksmith, sacristan. He emigrated to the United States, but over four years found no satisfaction there. Already the stomach trouble, which was to dog him all through life, was assailing him. He was only twenty-five when he offered himself for the Novitiate of the Congregation of the Holy Cross, young in years, old in the experience of the world and its bitterness.

From then till his death at the age of over ninety he suffered. He is associated with the great oratory of St. Joseph which stands on Mount Royal today. But his own little cell is far more moving. For his own devotion was given first not to Joseph but to Jesus on the Cross. In a lesser man the preoccupation with suffering might have been morbid and obsessional. In Brother André, as he now was, it meant a release of power. From childhood he had gazed with fascination at the crucifix. It was not an accident that he became a religious of the Holy Cross. He would brood for hours over his crucifix, sharing the agony of Christ with all his being, his muscles contracted, his tears streaming. From this developed his com-passion, his sym-pathy; for he had suffered with the Servant who was wounded for our transgressions and bruised for our iniquities. From this came the power of his prayers and words. "To pray well," he would say, "we must think of Jesus on the Cross. Impossible to have distractions when we see our Brother crucified"; and again, "If we thought that sin crucifies anew our Lord, ours would be real prayers"; and again, "Oh!

if only we loved the good God! If only we loved the good God as He has loved us!" From this sprang his ability to disregard his own sufferings; they were nothing beside his Lord's.

For he did suffer, acutely. Some suffering he laid upon himself, partly as discipline, partly that he might better enter into the way of the Cross. He slept little, and that often on the floor. He ate little, and that mostly an unedifying mixture of flour and water, or a few potatoes. If he slipped a few biscuits into his pocket, he generally forgot about them. Pain and illness were his all through life. He seldom complained, but in his last illness, the cry escaped him, "How I suffer, my God! How I suffer?" and told something of what he had been through all along. Alongside this was his spiritual suffering. There is evidence of strange spiritual torment, such as mystics seem often to experience. Where he was, queer noises might be heard. Sometimes he seemed to be engaged in physical struggle with unseen forces. One visitor paused outside the door of the cell in which he was alone, and heard his voice, "Go away, leave me alone! Go away!" Certainly he suffered temptations, of which the most acute was the temptation to pride in his achievements. "You know it is not my doing, it is God's. It is Saint Joseph who has done it," he would say. "I am only Saint Joseph's little dog." There is equally evidence of his isolation among his contemporaries, for though the common people heard him gladly, his colleagues did not understand him, and he was maligned as a charlatan or magician.

The astonishing thing is that Brother André was no grim ascetic, but a laughing saint bubbling over with a rich sense of humour. The face of the sufferer wore a smile, not as a mask to conceal suffering, but a smile of joy at the richness of a life which had overcome suffering. He loved to strike the pose of a boxer when meeting a friend, and would roar with laughter at the startled expressions on the faces of those he met and of passers-by. His words to those who came to consult him were salted with a keen wit, like his Master's. A girl, who as the seventh of her family was expected to show some special gift, came to consult him. "Pray to St. Joseph to let you have the gift of intelligence," was his advice. A woman who had been robbing his orchard came with a complaint of stomach-pains. "Rub yourself with this medal and try a diet of green apples." Another woman came, elegantly dressed in a precursor of the mini-skirt. "What's wrong with you is a phobia of getting entangled in your dress." A man with a painful leg, becoming impatient at the lack of progress, said that if nothing happened soon he would have it amputated. "Of course. Shall I call the surgeon now?" Brother André enjoyed his own wit, and recounted his experiences to his friends with great gusts of laughter.

But above all, he was a source of grace to many. He had a healer's hands. He attributed all his cures to St. Joseph; he would give St. Joseph's oil or St. Joseph's medal to rub the affected limb. Sometimes his word was enough. "Arise and walk," he would say, and men did arise and walk. A farmer came to him, terribly injured by one of his farm-machines. "Put aside your crutches," said Brother André, "and tomorrow you may resume your work." The farmer hobbled away. Next day he forced himself, in great pain, to follow the plough. That evening he returned with feet sorely swollen; his family told him that he was a fool, but he kept his faith. Next morning he woke up healed. Sometimes Brother André's presence was enough. Crowds rushed to hear him, to touch him, to let his shadow fall on them. A Protestant woman came to see him. She had no faith in St. Joseph and he spoke to her sharply. She went away in tears, and only after she had gone did she realize that she was healed. Sometimes it was his hands moving gently over a sufferer's eyes or limbs. "My hands produce the same effect as St. Joseph's medal," he remarked naïvely. He would be angry at the saying, but the truth was that St. Joseph's medal produced the same effect as his hands. Sometimes his prayers were the channel of healing at a distance. One remarkable story tells how a woman, herself a cripple, came to plead his intercession for her sister who was lying ill in the United States. She asked nothing for herself, but she and her sister were both cured. Another delightful episode relates to the opposition he encountered. He had enemies both ecclesiastic and civil, and appeals were made to the Bureau of Hygiene with a view to hampering his work. Brother André's answer was to cure the wife of one of the doctors who was persecuting him. Of course he was not always able to heal. But often, very often, he was. To those who came in idle curiosity he could be short and blunt. Towards those who came under a burden of sin, no time and trouble was too much. He would give hours to a reprobate drunkard. If he could win a soul from error, his whole energy would be absorbed. Another delightful story tells how he asked for eighteen copies of the life of Marie-Marthe Chambon, which he had just read, "to convert eighteen sinners".

The point of the life of Brother André is that he learned by suffering to heal suffering. "Were they to take me and kill me by cutting my body into small pieces, I would not mind," he said, "as long as the people were spared suffering." His power over suffering in others came from his conquest of it in himself. It came ultimately from his absorption in the way of Christ who showed that it is by suffering that God overpowers evil.

7

One of the great stories of transformation through suffering comes from Brazil, and deserves to be better known. Brazil was an area of bitter conflict between the indigenous Indians and the white immigrants. In the middle of the seventeenth century a company of settlers was massacred at a stream still called Rio del Mortes, or River of Death. From that time there was running warfare for 250 years. The settlers had two mottoes: "The only good Injun is a dead Injun" and "Shoot at sight, and ask questions afterwards."

Towards the end of the nineteenth century a remarkable man named Candedo Rondon was given charge of military operations against the Indians. Rondon was a soldier, an army colonel (he later rose to the rank of general) who had fought against the Indians and been wounded. He was also something of a mystic and saint. He knew, as many soldiers know, the futility of war. Two hundred and fifty years of warfare against the Indians had got nowhere. New methods must be tried. Rondon did an astonishing thing. Instead of pursuing the war, he formed a body

called the Indian Protective Service. His men were carefully picked
and trained. They were armed against wild animals. In relation
to the Indians they were given one rule, and that rule was absolute:
"Die if you must, but kill never." The government was engaged
in building roads and telegraph services for the benefit of the
whole people. It was Rondon's task to protect these services from
molestation and destruction. Rondon refused to use violence.
His weapons were persuasion and patience. There was some
destruction, but it was restored. Gradually the Indians were
persuaded that the new Service meant them good not harm. They
co-operated and became peaceable citizens.

Some, but not all. The fiercest of the Indian tribes, the Chavantes, remained recalcitrant. Rondon left them to themselves till
the main work of pacification and protection was over. Then he
turned his attention there. He sent in a first group of his men,
peaceable, refusing violence even in self-defence, knowing
what they were doing and facing. They were massacred. There
was a nation-wide demand for reprisals. Rondon remained calm;
he knew that his methods were right. He trained another thirty
men with meticulous care, and sent them in under his greatest
disciple Vanique. There they camped in the middle of hostile
murderers. Then they fanned out among the people. Their expressions of goodwill were met with suspicion, fear and hatred.
One day as they sat in their camp they saw an army of Chavantes
marching towards them with spears. Had they wished to resist
they were hopelessly outnumbered. Quietly, they resigned themselves to their Maker. Then they noticed that the spears were
pointed downwards, and blunted. The army halted. The spokes-
men advanced. They had come to sign a treaty of peace with
"the white Indians".

Of course all problems were not solved in a minute, and today
the Chavantes remain a violent and dangerous people. Yet in its
way this is a classical example of the way of the Cross in inter-
national and intergroup relations. Here was the refusal to meet
violence with violence, and the outreaching of an uncompromising love. Here was the suffering and death; no Cross no Crown.
Here was the victory through suffering, the power of God pouring

into the situation and transforming it. The victory is the more impressive because of the very violence of the Chavantes. Reinhold Niebuhr used to say that the methods of Jesus Christ, adopted by Gandhi, could work only when applied to a relatively humane opponent like the British. Some of us think this over-flattering to the British. But here is an example where the opponent was ruthless and was not transformed in the twinkling of an eye. Yet the Good Friday of Rondon's Service became Easter, and the thirty lives freely laid down brought to an end the useless wastage of hundreds and thousands of lives in centuries of war.

8

The Church still bears this witness triumphantly. Martin Luther King, the American Negro pastor, the man in the centre of the struggle for human rights in the U.S.A., has told the story of his pilgrimage to non-violence. In his teens he grew up to abhor segregation and the oppressive and barbarous acts which grew from it, and learned how racial injustice and economic injustice march hand in hand. Then as a student he read and reread Thoreau's *Essay on Civil Disobedience*; this established in his mind the idea of refusing to co-operate with an evil system. Next, as a theological student he was influenced by Walter Rauschen-busch's *Christianity and the Social Crisis* in its insistence that religion concerns not merely men's souls, but their bodies, and the economic and social conditions which scar the soul. Other influences crowded in, but Gandhi was, interestingly, the decisive factor in transforming his understanding of Christianity. He now saw that the ethics of Jesus applied to social as to individual relations. Christian love, humanistic non-violence, and Gandhian *Satyagraha* or truth-force came together in an outburst of power by atomic fusion, "Gandhi," he wrote, "was probably the first person in history to lift the love ethic of Jesus above mere inter-action between individuals to a powerful and effective social force on a large scale. Love for Gandhi was a potent instrument for social and collective transformation. It was in this Gandhian

emphasis on love and non-violence that I discovered the method
for social reform that I had been seeking for so many months."
Finally, Reinhold Niebuhr added a douche of realism, but his
misrepresentations of pacifism, so strange in a former pacifist,
were such that he failed to touch the essence of the position King
had reached. For "true pacifism is not unrealistic submission to
an evil power, as Niebuhr contends. It is rather a courageous
confrontation of evil by the power of love; in the faith that it is
better to be the recipient of violence than the inflicter of it, since
the latter only multiplies the existence of violence and bitterness
in the universe, while the former may develop a sense of shame
in the opponent, and thereby bring about a transformation and
change of heart."

King goes on to analyse the method of non-violent resistance.
First, it is not a method for cowards; it is not passive in the sense
of "do-nothing", only in its willingness to suffer aggression rather
than commit it; it may be passive physically, but it is strongly
active spiritually. Secondly, it does not seek to defeat or humiliate
the opponent, but to win his friendship and understanding.
Thirdly, it attacks the forces of evil not the people who happen
to be doing the evil. In America the conflict is between justice
and injustice, not Negro and white. Fourthly, the non-violent
resister will accept suffering without retaliation, because unearned
suffering is redemptive. So Gandhi: "Things of fundamental
importance to people are not secured by reason alone, but have
to be purchased with their suffering." Fifthly, the exponent of
Satyagraha avoids spiritual as well as physical violence. He cuts
the chain of hate by offering love instead, not of course a sentimental emotionalism, but an active outward-looking concern
for the neighbour's needs. Finally, non-violent resistance is
based on the conviction that the universe is on the side of justice.

This faith has been worked out in practice. In Montgomery,
Alabama, segregation was the rule. This was particularly resented
on the city's buses. Some seats were reserved for whites only.
Even if these were empty, Negroes had to stand. But if there were
more whites than reserved seats Negroes were forced to give up
their seats, and a fifteen-year-old schoolgirl named Claydette

Colvin was pulled off a bus, handcuffed and taken to prison because she refused to do so. When Rosa Parks, a woman of quiet speech, radiant personality and impeccable character, was arrested for the same offence, there was bound to be an explosion. In the event it was a non-violent explosion. The Negroes simply refused to use the buses. A pool of cars helped the elderly and infirm. Mostly they just walked. The spirit of heroic self-sacrifice is exemplified by two stories of elderly women. A driver stopped by one. "Jump in, grandmother," he said. "You don't need to walk." "I'm not walking for myself," she said, "I'm walking for my children and grandchildren." She walked on. The other was asked after several weeks of walking whether she was not tired. She replied, "My feets is tired, but my soul is at rest." It took twelve months' walking before the buses were de-segregated. But the case was won. It led to an outburst of violence and bomb-outrages by fanatical whites. But Martin Luther King addressed his people: "We must not return violence under any condition. I know this is difficult advice to follow, especially since we have been the victims of no less than ten bombings. But this is the way of Christ; it is the way of the cross. We must somehow believe that unearned suffering is redemptive." There was no retaliation. The disturbances ceased. In a few weeks the transport system was functioning normally and people of both races rode side by side wherever they pleased.

Martin Luther King has since trodden his master's road to the end.

7

The Gospel of Suffering

1

This world has often been called a vale of tears. It is more than that, much more. Gladness and sorrow mingle together.

> Joy and woe are woven fine,
> A clothing for the soul divine.

Yet for all the gladness, there *is* sorrow, there *is* suffering, nature *is* red in tooth and claw, the whole creation *is* groaning and travailing. We who seek to worship God with mind as well as heart and soul and strength cannot fail to ask Why? This is what John Stuart Mill called "the impossible problem of reconciling infinite benevolence and justice with infinite power in the Creator of such a world as this". So Browning:

> Wherefore should any evil hap to man—
> From ache of flesh to agony of soul—
> Since God's All-mercy mates All-potency?
> Nay, why permits He evil to Himself—
> Man's sin, accounted such? Suppose a world
> Purged of all pain, with fit inhabitant—
> Man pure of evil in thought, word, and deed—
> Were it not well? Then, wherefore otherwise?

We cannot evade this question.

Broadly speaking, three answers have been given.

The first is the dualistic answer of later Zoroastrianism. Good and evil are both ultimate powers in the universe; they are not to be explained; they are themselves the explanation. There is nothing unreasonable about this; to that qualified pessimism which we call worldly wisdom it might seem eminently reasonable. The only snag is that it offers a strictly amoral system, and this is certainly not what its propounders intend. For if good and evil are both ultimate, then one is not more ultimate than the other, and there is no reason why we should back good rather than evil. The Zoroastrian is in the position of Orwell's dictator who proclaimed that all animals are equal, but some are more equal than others. We cannot have it both ways: either good is ultimate and evil is not, in which case we have not explained evil, or both are ultimate, in which case they are descriptive not moral terms, and there is no moral reason for supporting one rather than the other.

We may of course calculate that the forces of "good" are stronger than the forces of "evil". But we may equally calculate that the forces of "evil" are stronger, as in the (Christian) limerick:

> The world made a lovely beginning,
> But was spoiled at the start by man's sinning.
> We know that the story
> Will end with God's glory—
> But at present the other side's winning.

In a strict dualism we do not know that the story will end with God's glory, and no moral obloquy attaches to the calculation that at present the other side's winning and that we will therefore back it. Further, the thing is psychologically wrong. "Evil, be thou my good" is a state of mind we all know. Even one of Ovid's heroines can cry

> I see and approve the better course,
> I follow the worse.

"The good that I would I do not, the evil that I would not, that I do." But, to the strict dualist "Evil, be thou my good" makes no sense, no psychological sense, that is, for it attributes a moral ultimacy to good. Dualism neither gives a satisfactory psychological explanation of good and evil nor a satisfactory philosophical account.

The second explanation we have met among the Stoics. It is also to be found in Indian religious thought. This is the view that pain and evil are illusion. This is a common form of pseudo-explanation; it merely pushes the problem one stage further back. A limerick will again illustrate the point:

> There was a faith-healer of Deal,
> Who said, "Although pain isn't real,
>   When I sit on a pin
>   And it punctures my skin,
> I dislike what I fancy I feel."

Evil may be illusion, but is not the illusion itself evil? Why the illusion? If we say that it is an illusion to suppose that the illusion is evil, we are involved in an infinite regress. If we offer some other explanation, then we are offering an alternative to the view that evil is illusion.

These two are impossible explanations. The third, however difficult, is more satisfactory than these. This is the Christian view. It says that God who is good makes a world which is good (there are linguistic problems here, but they do not invalidate the picture). But that world has been from the first a world which may go wrong. Why? Because the highest point of God's creation is free beings with freedom of will and freedom of choice. If this freedom of choice is real and meaningful, it is a freedom to choose God or not to choose God, to choose right or to choose wrong (again linguistic problems enter). Furthermore, it must follow that a wrong choice will lead to wrong results, or there is no real choice; if the suitor won Portia whichever casket he chose, then there would be no real choice. Freedom of choice is possible only in a world which contains the potentiality of evil as well as the potentiality of good. This is superbly put in Aldous Huxley's anti-Utopia *Brave New World*, in the conversation between the Savage and Mustapha Mond.

> "But I don't want comfort. I want God, I want poetry, I want real danger, I want freedom, I want goodness, I want sin."
> "In fact," said Mustapha Mond, "you're claiming the right to be unhappy."
> "All right then," said the Savage defiantly, "I'm claiming the right to be unhappy."
> "Not to mention the right to grow old and ugly and impotent;

the right to have syphilis and cancer; the right to have too little to eat; the right to be lousy; the right to live in constant apprehension of what may happen tomorrow; the right to catch typhoid; the right to be tortured by unspeakable pains of every kind." There was a long silence.

"I claim them all," said the Savage at last.

Mustapha Mond shrugged his shoulders. "You're welcome," he said.

Of course this is not the whole story. Nature was red in tooth and claw before man came on the scene, and if we succumb to a form of the pathetic fallacy which invests animals with our own sentiments, we may not go to the other extreme which suggests that the fox enjoys being hunted, or that the bird confronted with the cat is impervious to pain and fear. We can, however, say that the possibility of moral choice and the faculty of sentience seem to go together. We do not accuse a mountain of immorality (though a child may say "Naughty chair" of a recalcitrant object). But we rebuke dogs, and expect them to conform to standards we impose upon them, and we admire the mother-bird which pretends to be wounded in order to divert a snake from its young. Paul, as we have seen, in the great vision of the eighth chapter of *Romans*, looks on the whole creation as awry. But suffering is not nicely related to sin. The most we can say is that a world in which beings are free to choose good is a world in which beings are free to choose evil, that if they choose evil things will go wrong, for themselves and for others, that it is a world in which the innocent will suffer. The Christian faith does not tidily tie up the ends of explanation; we grope in twilight, dimly discerning that a moral world must be a world of this nature. But the Christian faith shows how the fact of suffering can be taken up and used in the purposes of God.

There is another fact of some importance; this is the fact that there is a problem. In an eloquent lecture J. S. Whale said of Man: "He thinks he was not made to die. Like Cleopatra, he has immortal longings in him. If he is meant to perish, as 'sheep or goats that nourish a blind life within the brain', why is he tortured with dreams, and creative heroisms, with noble disinterestedness and above all, with love, which makes bereavement his immemorial agony? If Death is the Everlasting No, striking him down to dust inexorably at the last, why is there an Everlasting Yea in his heart?" If there were not meaning to life, suffering would not be a problem, it would be a fact like any other. When we see it as a problem, as we do, however humanistic or atheistic our professions, we are viewing it against the background of a good and loving God. There is an old Latin tag, *Si deus est, unde malum? Si non est, unde bonum?* "If God exists, where does evil come from? If not, where does good come from?"

Suffering then has its place in the world of God's children.

2

The second great truth about suffering is that it can make us more sensitive to others. Shelley justified poetry by claiming that it "strengthens the faculty which is the organ of the moral nature of man in the same manner as exercise strengthens a limb". "The great secret of morals is love; or a going out of our nature, and an identification of ourselves with the beautiful which exists in thought, action, or person not our own. A man to be greatly good must imagine intensely and comprehensively; he must put himself in the place of another and of many others; the pains and pleasures of his species must become his own. The great instrument of moral good is the imagination; and poetry administers to the effect of acting upon the cause." Shelley also wrote in *Julian and Maddalo*

> Most wretched men
> Are cradled into poetry by wrong,
> They learn in suffering what they teach in song.

Compassion involves passion; sympathy implies pathos; before we can suffer with another we must know suffering for ourselves. So only can we follow Walt Whitman: "I do not ask the wounded person how he feels, I myself become the wounded person."

Of course it does not follow that those who suffer become inevitably more imaginative, more sensitive, more loving. On the contrary they may become hard and bitter; they may set up shields and barriers to protect themselves from being hurt even at second hand; they may take a malicious delight when others are hurt as they have been hurt. There is an element of choice. But just as Toynbee has claimed that an element of challenge is needful for a civilization to emerge, though if there is no response the embryonic civilization may be crushed, just as a man who learns too easily will seldom be a good teacher because he does not understand his students' problems, so the man who will help his fellows at the deepest level, must know suffering. When in Shakespeare's play the news of the massacre of Macduff's family is drawn from the reluctant Ross, young, callow Malcolm offers words of conventional comfort, which Macduff flings aside with, "He has no children." Suffering is a challenge. It may embitter us; or we may turn it to the service of God and man. Tenderness is after all a capacity for being hurt. A Chinese patient said of a missionary doctor, "He took my sickness into his own heart."

There is a wonderful story told by the bushmen of the Kalahari. Mantis, the primal praying-mantis, is the spirit of creation. His supreme creation was the Eland. But Mantis's children watched him secretly, and one day when he was away they killed the Eland and ate him. Mantis was desolate. He went to the scene of the killing and there he found on a bush the indigestible gall of the Eland; he had found the bitterness of creation. He told the gall that he would jump on it and pierce it through; the gall answered that if he did it would burst open and cover him. Mantis was tempted to go away after his children. "Father, if it be possible, let this cup pass from me; none the less not as I will, but as Thou wilt." He resisted the temptation, leaped upon the gall, pierced it through, and was swamped in bitter darkness. Here as he groped unseeing his grip suddenly lighted upon an ostrich feather. He used this to wipe away the gall from his face. He had passed through darkness into light, and flung the feather into the sky to be the moon and to light others in their darkness. For there is suffering in creation, and there is light in darkness, but we cannot see the light until we have known the darkness.

In this way God does not always remove suffering from our path. Paul had his "thorn in the flesh" (2 *Cor.* 12.7); exactly what it was is disputed, but clearly it was some sort of physical disability. Three times he prayed that it might be removed from him. God's answer to his prayer was that it was better not to remove it, but to give him the power to use it. It is this that leads Paul to his triumphant outburst: "Therefore I glory in my infirmities." Christianity does not negate suffering, but turns it into a positive force. So did the great Persian weavers take a mistake, and weave it into a new, more glorious pattern.

Teilhard de Chardin has shown something of how this may be. The world, he says, is in a state of growth. We are like the leaves and blossoms on some great tree—not like hothouse flowers cosseted and sheltered—and must expect the buffetings attendant on growth. Sufferers reflect this austere but noble condition. Furthermore, by the nature of their destiny they are driven out of themselves. It is for them to raise the world above and beyond immediate enjoyment towards an ever more exalted light. Suffering is potential energy. In suffering is concealed the world's power of ascension. The whole problem is to liberate it by making it conscious of what it means and what it can achieve. So the world's pain could become the world's conscience. Jesus on the cross is not defeated but victorious, not passive but active, bearing towards God the progress of the universal advance.

These words were written by a wise Christian:

"Once I thought that I had been wounded as no man ever had. Because I felt this I vowed to write this book. But long before I began the book the wound had healed. Since I had sworn to fulfil my task I reopened the horrible wound.

"Let me put it another way. . . . Perhaps in opening the wound, my own wound, I closed other wounds, other people's wounds. Something dies, something blossoms. To suffer in ignorance is horrible. To suffer deliberately, in order to understand the nature of suffering and abolish it forever, is quite another matter. The Buddha had one fixed thought in mind all his life, as we know. It was to eliminate human suffering.

"Suffering *is* unnecessary. But one has to suffer before he is

I

able to realize that this is so. It is only then, moreover, that the true significance of human suffering becomes clear. At the last desperate moment—when one can suffer no more!—something happens which is in the nature of a miracle. The great open wound which was draining the blood of life closes up, the organism blossoms like a rose. One is free at last. . . ."

Ah! Must—Designer Infinite!—
Ah, Must Thou char the wood ere Thou canst limn
With it?

The answer to Francis Thompson's question is "Yes."

3

But suffering does more than transform us. It transforms others. A simple story, less dramatic than some we have told, may serve as an illustration. It comes from the American missionary-preacher Stanley Jones. In a land where "face" matters a man was giving a lecture. One of the questioners accused him of being a liar. Instead of flaring up, or retiring into a protective shell, he took the accusation patiently and fairly. The incident passed by. But that night one of the audience could not sleep. He had a quarrel with another, and the lecturer's patient willingness to suffer taunts was searing his conscience. At 3 a.m. he got up and went to his enemy, talked over their estrangement with him, asked, received and gave forgiveness. Next day in church he stood up and asked forgiveness of those whom he had offended with his tongue. His attitude spread to others. Thirty-four quarrels were settled that morning.

Another example, in this case from a social relationship, is the industrial strike. When an industrial strike succeeds it does not succeed merely or even primarily through economic pressure. It succeeds because the men, in protest against injustice, are ready to suffer and to sacrifice. This convinces others of their sincerity and so draws attention to the reality of the injustice. For a man does not imperil his secure employment and reduce his income to strikers' pay for a frivolous cause. This is the real power behind the strike.

The life of George Fox offers cogent instances. "Here is gospel for thee," he said to one of his persecutors, "here is my hair and there is my cheek and here is my shoulders," and as he recorded later "the truth came so over him that he grew loving". He wrote in his *Journal* (2, 338): "And there was never any persecution that came but we saw it was for good, and we looked upon it to be good, as from God; and there was never any prisons or sufferings that I was in but still it was for the bringing multitudes more out of prison." So he advised his followers: "Look not at your sufferings, but at the power of God, and that will bring some good out in all your sufferings; and your imprisonments will reach to the prisoned, that the persecutor prisons in himself." For Fox believed that there was "that of God" in every man which could be reached and touched. His actions were always designed to touch that, to bring a man to his senses and his true self. It did not always succeed in the short run, but time and again it did, and it always stood a better chance of success than anger and violence.

The most obvious example of this is martyrdom. We must not give slick explanations. Tacitus tells us that the mob who watched the persecution of the Christians under Nero came to sympathize with the Christians and feel pity with them, not because of their bearing but because the excessive cruelty used by Nero led the onlookers to feel that this was sadism not just punishment. Marcus Aurelius regarded the courage of Christians in face of death as pig-headed obstinacy. Others were moved by Christian witness. Paul himself no doubt by the bearing of Stephen; his immediate response was a campaign of bitter persecution, and it does not need a profound psychologist to see that this was directed against his own inner doubts and questionings; on the Damascus road he had the vision of Jesus which Stephen had had as he died; thereafter he set himself to follow Stephen's steps. Tertullian was another. In our own day there is testimony enough of hardened Nazis or Communists being stirred to their depths by the courage of martyrs. Whatever the explanation, it is factually true, whether in Rome or Scilli or Lyons, in Berlin or Warsaw, in Madagascar or Bonny, that the blood of the martyrs has proved the seed of the Church. Kierkegaard, that lonely agonized thinker, who saw and felt more deeply than most, made a well-known distinction between the tyrant and the martyr. Both constrain others, the tyrant, ambitious to rule, by the power he wields, the martyr, obedient to God, by what he suffers. So the tyrant dies and his rule ends; the martyr dies and his rule begins. The Church, wrote Christopher Dawson, "wins not by majorities but by martyrs and the Cross is her victory". The key-word is "wins".

It is important to see that creative suffering is never undertaken for its own sake, but always in obedience to God, always, that is to say, as sacrifice. For there are two attitudes to suffering which are sterile. The first is the unnatural enjoyment of suffering. It is a form of masochism, a misdirection of our sexual energy, and because it is a misdirection of creative power it cannot itself be creative. Creative suffering is voluntary, but it is not self-inflicted. "For this reason," said Jesus, "the Father loves me, because I lay down my life, that I may take it again. No one takes it from me, but I lay it down of my own accord. I have power to lay it down, and I have power to take it again; this charge I have received from my Father" (*John* 10.17-18). No doubt he forced the issue by the cleansing of the Temple. But the Cross was not suicide, and it was not undertaken out of self-torment but out of obedience: "Lo, I have come to do Thy will" (*Hebr.* 10.9). This is creative suffering. "Blessed are the meek", is not slave-morality, as Nietzsche alleged. "If this is slave-morality," wrote Bertrand Russell, no friend to Christianity, "then every soldier of fortune who endures the rigours of a campaign, and every rank-and-file politician who works hard at electioneering is to be accounted a slave. But in fact, in every genuinely co-operative enterprise, the follower is psychologically no more a slave than the leader."

The other sterile attitude is to use suffering compulsively for one's own purposes. On a small scale in the family circle this too often happens—the mother or other member of the family who by word or look pleads her self-sacrifice in order to tyrannize over her children is only one example. There is a self-centred unselfishness which is self-defeating. Worldly wisdom, as it happens, has scarcely realized the sheer effectiveness of non-violent action in public life. The sort of worldly wisdom which pursues selfish ends publicly usually leans to violent means. Even if a readiness to suffer be used for selfish ends it may not be wholly sterile. At least it is not destructive. At best it may transform the sufferer.

There is a fact here which Christians must believe. This world is God's world, however fallen, and it will work only in God's way. In this world violence breeds violence. A classical example took place in Nigeria in 1966. There was a situation of political tyranny imposed by corruption and violence. It was clear that the violence used by S. L. Akintola and his party, backed by the Sardauna of Sokoto in the north, was, humanly speaking, bound to provoke a violent reaction. When Akintola and the Sardauna were assassinated by a group of Ibo soldiers, a great wave of relief swept over the country, and many normally sane and balanced people felt that the violence used was fully justified. But those who looked further knew that the only lesson violence teaches is more violence. The January "coup" was followed with grim inevitability by the July mutiny and the anti-Ibo riots in the North, and they in turn by anti-Hausa riots in the East. The sumless tale of sorrow piles up. When Jesus said to Peter, "Put up your sword into its place, for all who take the sword will perish by the sword" (*Matt*. 26.52) he meant exactly what he said, and he was speaking not to an aggressor, but to an honest man who was seeking to defend by violence an innocent man from wrongful arrest; as Tertullian was to say, he thereby cursed the works of the sword for ever. If we are Christians we may not use violence, however just the cause, because no matter how effective it may seem to be in the short run (the January "coup"), in the long run it will add immeasurably to the sum of violence.

What Jesus shows is another way. It is a law of life. James calls it "the royal law" (2.8), the law of love, the law of liberty, the perfect law. This is the way of the cross. It is the confrontation of evil, not with evil but with good (*Matt*. 5.39; *Rom*. 12, 21). It involves the acceptance of sacrificial suffering; this is what Jesus means when he says that any disciple of his must take up his own cross. This is God's way of changing the world; this is the way of redeeming, transforming love. It is not worldly wisdom.

The preaching of the Cross is foolishness to Greeks who seek after wisdom (1 *Cor.* 1.22-5), but because it is God's folly it is wiser than men. No matter how ineffective it may seem to be in the short run (Good Friday), in the long run, through sacrificial obedience the power of God floods into the world. If we do not believe this, we do not—effectively—believe in God. If we make our calculations leaving God out, we do not—effectively—believe in God.

"The only right of the Christian," said Luther, "is suffering and the Cross." William Penn, in his *No Cross, No Crown*, produced in prison, wrote: "We must either renounce to believe what the Lord Jesus hath told us, that whosoever doth not bear his cross and come after Him cannot be His disciple, or admitting that for truth, conclude that generality of Christendom do miserably deceive and disappoint themselves in the great business of Christianity and their own salvation." "Oh how great a part of Christianity is it to understand and rightly bear the cross! Oh! little, too little, do many honest Christians think how much of their most excellent obedience consisteth in child-like, holy suffering." The words are Richard Baxter's from *Dying Thoughts*. Campbell Morgan once said: "The Church has won Christ's victories by sacrifice, and in no other way. It is never until she is wounded that she wins." We "share abundantly in Christ's sufferings" (2 *Cor.* 1.5).

4

And Christ shares in ours.

Christianity does not offer an intellectual explanation of suffering. The Christian faith offers a God who shares in our suffering. The assertion that God was in Christ reconciling the world to Himself (2 *Cor.* 5.19) is the central affirmation of the Christian believer.

God suffers. "In spite of much Church doctrine," Wheeler Robinson, "an impassible God is as impossible as a docetic Christ." The Church rightly rejected the Docetists who maintained that Christ did not truly suffer. The Church also rejected the

Patripassians, but not for the reasons commonly supposed. About A.D. 180 Praxeas taught that the Father suffered on the Cross in the person of the Son; he later added that he suffered by sympathy. Noetus developed this doctrine, and in developing it obliterated all distinction between the Father and the Son, arguing that the Father was born and lived and died as a man. It was this that the Church rejected as heresy, not the teaching that God suffers, but the teaching that the Father is identical with the Son. We cannot think of the God revealed in Jesus Christ as one of those remote, indifferent deities of the Epicureans, who, in Tennyson's words,

> haunt
> The lucid interspace of world and world,
> Where never creeps a cloud, or moves a wind,
> Nor ever falls the least white star of snow,
> Nor ever lowest roll of thunder moans,
> Nor sound of human sorrow ever mounts to mar
> Their sacred everlasting calm.

We face the living God, active within His world. "My Father," said Jesus, "is still at work" (*John* 5.17), and Von Hügel once remarked, "Suffering is the purest form of activity, perhaps the only form of activity." More than that, God is Love, and Love means self-sacrifice. Love bears all things. God loves the world so much that he gave.

The artists and poets have realized this. The Italian painter who pictured the nails going through the hands of Jesus and through the wood of the Cross into the hands of the Father behind knew what he was about. So did the Psalmist who sang

> Whither shall I go from thy Spirit?
>   Or whither shall I flee from thy presence?
> If I ascend to heaven, thou art there!
>   If I make my bed in Sheol, thou art there!

> (*Ps.* 139.7–8)

So did William Blake when he wrote in Milton (2, 35):

> For God himself enters Death's Door always with those that enter
> And lays down in the Grave with them, in Visions of Eternity.

and again:

> God is within and without: he is even in the depths of hell.

So did Browning in *Balaustion's Adventure*:

> I think this is the authentic sign and seal
> Of Godship, that it ever waxes glad,
> And more glad, until gladness blossoms, bursts,
> Into a rage to suffer for mankind,
> And recommence at sorrow: drops like seed . . .
> And thence rise, tree-like grow through pain to joy,
> More joy and most joy,—do man good again.

There is a story from the late Middle Ages. Up in the Vosges mountains plague was raging, or rather plagues, for they were of many forms, all of them grievous, none worse than the so-called St. Anthony's fire, which caused the lower limbs to swell till they became green and gangrenous, and the patients eventually died in agony. There was little that human help could do, but the hermits who lived in the mountains offered what care and consolation they might. To this community in agony came Matthias Grünewald, the painter, and for them he painted the fearful crucifixion which hangs in Colmar today, showing Christ contorted as their bodies were contorted, agonized as they were agonized, his limbs swollen like theirs. The hermits who nursed the sufferers through their last hours set them down where they could see this picture, and for some at least of them it meant the certainty that God was with them sharing in their agony, and could in His eternal and inscrutable purpose give meaning to the meaningless, turn pain to joy and bring life out of death.

God suffers. The Lamb is slain from the foundation of the world (*Rev.* 13.8); whether the words of the seer are rightly so taken or not, the truth is sure. "There was a cross in the heart of God before there was one planted on the green hill outside Jerusalem," wrote Dinsmore, "and, now that the cross of wood has been taken down, the one in the heart of God abides, and it will remain so long as there is one sinful soul for whom to suffer."

Christianity does not explain the mystery of suffering, still less explain it away. It proclaims that suffering does not separate

us from God, and that as he calls us to share in the work of
redemption, he calls us to accept the suffering through which the
work is fulfilled.

A gloomy cross stood on the path I trod,
 I needs must lift it, would I onward go;—
On it was written clear, "*The Will of God.*"
 Gazing, I wept and trembled, bending low.

For much I dreaded what might be behind;
 Till Faith came forward, with her words of cheer,
"Why weepest thou, O thou of doubtful mind?
 Arise and take thy cross! What dost thou fear?"

She raised me up and pointed, when, behold!
 The cross that terrified had passed away,
And there, with "*Love*" inscribed in burnished gold,
 Another stood, which shone resplendently.

Awhile I carried it, with wondering awe;
 Its glory shone, a light upon my road,
Till, looking at the other side, I saw
 The words which I had feared, "*The Will of God.*"

I looked at Faith; she smiled,—"I did but move
 The cross around and show the other name;
Behind the Will there always lies the Love;
 The Will and Love with God are but the same."